TOMORROW'S
CHRISTIAN

By the same author

Tomorrow's Parish
McCrimmons, Essex (1983)
(Also published in German, Thai, Chinese and Malay)

God and the Aquarian Age
McCrimmons, Essex (1990)

A New Framework for Christian Belief
John Hunt Publishing Ltd, Hampshire (2002)

A Reason for Living and Hoping: A Christian Appreciation of the Emerging New Era of Consciousness.
St Paul's Publishing, London (2002)

The God Shift: Our Changing Perception of the Ultimate Mystery
The Liffey Press, Dublin (2004)

TOMORROW'S CHRISTIAN

A new framework for Christian living

Adrian B. Smith

Author of *A New Framework for Christian Belief*

BOOKS

Winchester, UK
New York, USA

Copyright © 2005 O Books
Deershot Lodge, Park Lane, Ropley, Hants, SO24 OBE, UK.
Tel: +44 (0) 1962 773768 Fax: +44 (0) 1962 773769
E-mail: office@johnhunt-publishing.com
www.O-books.net

U.S.A. and Canada
Books available from:
NBN,
15200 NBN Way
Blue Ridge Summit, PA 17214, U.S.A.
Email: custserv@nbnbooks.com
Tel: 1 800 462 6420
Fax: 1 800 338 4550

Text: © 2005 Adrian B. Smith
Design: Text set in Chaparral by Jim Weaver Design,
Basingstoke, UK
Cover design: Krave Ltd, London

ISBN 1 903816 97 1

A CIP catalogue record for this book is available from the
British Library.

Printed by Maple-Vail Book Manufacturing Group, USA

Contents

Introduction

Christians are increasingly feeling a disjunction between the beliefs with which they were brought up and the reality of the world as they experience it today.

Those who feel the need to be true to their experience in order that the religious dimension of their lives is not being lived as a falsehood, appear to follow one of three paths.

There are those who are feeling increasingly insecure in an area upon which their lives have always been grounded. Their traditional understanding of their faith has given them a foundation upon which they have built their values, according to which they have made their moral judgments. With challenges to this framework now being made by those both outside and within the Church, they are feeling like a small boat that has slipped its anchor. Their way of facing this is to take more literally and as absolutes the truths that have guided them till now, expressed particularly in the word of God in the Bible. These people are variously labeled by others as Conservatives, Fundamentalists, Literalists, Creationists. They are a minority – but a growing minority – in all denominations. Their counterpart is found in the Jewish, Muslim, and Hindu religions. They give an unquestioning obedience to their interpretation of the revelation in their Scriptures. Whether the fundamentalist be Christian, Jew, Muslim, or Hindu, their respective Holy Scriptures have become their object of faith, their God.

A second group is moving from an intellectual basis of beliefs and Church practice to search for an experiential religion, inviting into their spiritual lives an emotional dimension. They would describe themselves as Charismatics. Their key word would be religious "experience," describing both the evident presence of the Holy Spirit in their lives and their enjoyment of its community dimension.

The third group has become disillusioned. The realities of today's world, its science, its increasing human control over nature, its evolutionary theories of our origins, its ever-changing ethical values, all these cause them to regard their previous religious beliefs, traditionally expressed, as no longer tenable and their religious practices as hollow. They gave comfort and made sense to a previous generation – and to themselves in their own childhood – but contribute little to explain the world as they experience it today. Some of this group respond by opting out of Church membership, regarding it as a contemporary irrelevance. Others, whom we name here "Tomorrow's Christians," struggle to bring together in a meaningful way, traditional Christianity on the one hand and, on the other, a contemporary, nourishing understanding and expression of it.

It is my prediction that the first group will grow, especially in Latin America, Africa, and Asia, and will take possession of the Church to retain it as a secure haven. This will unintentionally cause a new form of Church to come to birth in the West. The second group is in a transitional phase from a previously private me-and-God faith, more concerned with observance than with interiorization, to a deeper spiritual faith expressing itself in more interior practices such as various forms of contemplative meditation. This minority group will grow and have an increasing influence on the future direction of Christian living, often outside official Church structures.

The present book is offered as a help to the third group to bridge the gap between their experience of the contemporary world and traditional Christian belief and practice. One might ask how the third group came about. It is not such an obscure view today that we are presently embarked upon one of the greatest consciousness shifts that have been made in human history. The first such happened during the few hundred years before and after 500 BCE and gave rise to the world religions as we have them today. It has been termed the Axial Period, a profound cultural change. Our present times have been named the Second Axial Period, comparable to the first for the intensity and depth of the change that is coming about. Nevertheless, it is subtle and is not perceived as such by the majority of people because it is not evident on the surface of everyday life. Signs of it are sometimes commented upon, but the "big picture" toward which the signs point is not within the awareness of most people.

The Big Picture is so big that it encompasses a new perception of the supreme mystery, which we name "God." It calls for a review of our relationship to our fellow human beings with all their differences of faith, color, culture, and a new relationship to the planet we inhabit. The way we live as Christians, our attitudes, our practices, the way we understand Christian doctrine, our prayer life – all these are affected by the great consciousness shift taking place.

Philosophers refer to our present time as that of Post-modernism, whose characteristics are the current critique of our present culture, of rationalism, of science, indeed of all certainty and of objective truth. All that till now has underpinned our western culture is in the melting pot. These are not comfortable times.

❦

At the close of each chapter I have offered some questions for reflection. However, there is a danger in going directly from the text to the questions that the matter stays in the head. It is wise, therefore, after reading the text to pause and ponder in our hearts before moving on. Some entirely different but more appropriate questions may then arise.

If the chapters are used by a group, the questions might be discussion-starters. (See Appendix for a suggested way of using the material in a group.)

Throughout, I have used the present tense in describing tomorrow's Christian because many people are there already!

one

a questioning person ...

... can say with St Paul: "When I was a child my speech, feelings, and thinking were all those of a child: now that I am grown up I have no more use for childish ways"

(1 Corinthians 13:11).

There was a time, not so long ago, when Christians were expected to believe the truths of their faith as propounded by the clergy. The expectation existed on both sides. Christians felt that matters theological were too complicated for scrutiny and that revelation was too holy for examination. The clergy, for their part, felt that on their shoulders was placed the responsibility of handing on faithfully to the laity the doctrinal teaching they had received in Bible School, Theological College, or Seminary.

The laity were dissuaded from, if not actually forbidden from, questioning the religious teaching they received. Times have changed.

Most of us have received the sort of education that encourages us to question all aspects of life and, in particular, to question the authority of those "in authority", whether in the secular or religious domain.

Beliefs, teaching, rules of conduct are no more than signposts pointing us in the direction of the Ultimate Reality to which religions give the name "God." We meet that Reality, not only in the external signs, but in our "still center," the center of our Being, because our Being is what we share with God who is Being.

Most of us first met the signposts as children, in Sunday school or Catechism class, and from our earliest experience of churchgoing. And we would probably claim to have matured, to have questioned, to have discarded or re-formulated our earlier beliefs in keeping with our personal experience and growth in knowledge. As did St Paul: "When I was a child, my speech, feelings, and thinking were all those of a child; now that I am grown up, I have no more use for childish ways" (1 Corinthians 13:11). Nevertheless, that understanding of things religious that was implanted in us in our childhood sank deep into our consciousness. At the intellectual level we may have moved on, but at the deepest, gut level awesome images of God and fears of eternal damnation and feelings of guilt may still linger.

One of the signposts that we carry since childhood is the Creed. For tomorrow's Christian the Creeds – in whichever form – present a problem because each was composed, not as a compendium of faith, but for a particular purpose in a culture other than our own. The manner in which their truths are stated does not ring true with our own experience. People address this problem in two ways. They either keep silent when the rest of the congregation is reciting the Creed or they join in, realizing that they are not thereby affirming their belief in the literal meaning of each of the statements, but with the sense that in joining in they are in communion with generations of Christians who have used this statement in an attempt to express the ineffable. Either way, there is an awareness of a gap between the formulation of the ancient Creeds and the manner in which we understand religious truths today.

Divine Truth is absolute and unchanging. It can never be grasped by us humans in its entirety. Dogmas, whether they are religious, political, or scientific, arise out of the erroneous belief that thoughts can encapsulate Reality or the Truth.

Dogmas are limited expressions of aspects of the Truth. Regarded as a definitive expression, they can become an intellectual prison. (There are those who love their prison because it gives them security.) When we speak of "the Truth" it means no more than the way we collectively understand Reality at this present time. St Paul acknowledges this in his hymn to Love (1 Corinthians 13): "Our gifts of knowledge and of inspired messages are only partial" (v.9), "What I know now is only partial: then it will be complete – as complete as God's knowledge of me" (v.12).

No Church can claim to possess the fullness of Truth. We can only grapple with partial truths. Behind each of our attempts to express Divine Truth there lie experiences, personal and thus unique to each of us, that neither a word nor a phrase can fully describe. Words like "salvation," "grace," "revelation" will convey something different to each person because they refer to personal and unfathomable experiences of others as well as of ourselves.

matters for pondering or discussion

1   Can you, like St Paul, say honestly that you have discarded your childish "feelings and thinking" on religious matters?

2   If there is some deep residue of early indoctrination, can you name it? Can you challenge it?

3   Do you have the possibility of meeting with others of a like religious mind with whom you can share your thoughts and feelings and so be helped to unravel them?

4   If not, can you see a possibility of setting up such a faith-support group in your area?

two

a kingdom person ...

... believes that the Church is at the service of a greater good: God's reign.

The key to understanding the changes that are currently taking place in Church life and thinking, which will shape the Church of tomorrow, is found in the shift – a truly paradigm shift – that is already occurring: a shift from a Christianity which is Church-oriented to a Christianity which is Kingdom-oriented.

Jesus spoke of humanity's fulfillment with the metaphor, "Kingdom of God," meaning by that, a life which is ordered by interior, spiritual power rather than by external, human-controlled power. In the context of the Palestine of his own times, Jesus was illustrating, through his own life and teaching, how God would run the world if God, not Caesar, sat on the imperial throne.

The Good News of Jesus the Christ is about our ultimate human fulfillment. His preaching was not in order to establish a new religion, nor even to found a Church as we know it today. Yet it was not a message about the "next life": it was firmly grounded in our present life. Although the whole of creation has been moving toward this destiny since its inception, it was only after several million years of humanity's existence upon this planet that human consciousness became aware that there was indeed a destiny. With the coming among us of Jesus the Christ, this destiny was made known to us as God's design for creation. "In past times mankind was not told this secret, but God has revealed it now by the Spirit to his holy apostles and martyrs. The secret is that by means of the gospel the Gentiles have a part with the Jews in God's blessings; they are members of the same body and share in the promise that God made through Christ Jesus" (Ephesians 3:5-6).

For those of us who have been brought up within the Christian tradition it is difficult to appreciate that Jesus' "Good News" was not about the Church but about the Kingdom, the destiny of the whole of humanity. (In fact, only twice is the word "church" found on the lips of Jesus, both recorded in Matthew's Gospel [16:18 and 18:17] and from their context many scholars believe these two passages were added later, after a Church had come into existence.)

The phrase "Kingdom of God," as an expression of the vision of Jesus, has lost its appeal to us of the western world in the twenty-first century. The word "Kingdom" conjures up images of knights and castles and implies a masculine God. Since Jesus was not speaking of a geographical location, a happier expression might be the "Reign of God," or had he been employing today's language he might have spoken instead of the Christ Age, or the Age of Universality, or the New Civilization of Love, all of which are more meaningful expressions in a world where there are few kingdoms remaining. However, while allowing for its inadequacy, I will continue to use the term Kingdom of God because of its biblical origin.

Jesus announced by action and word, in terms of the Kingdom, that God had a plan, a vision, a design for humanity and that with Jesus' own coming that promised new era was already being manifested.

It was coming true in his person because he lived with the belief that the Kingdom was present for the asking if only people would be open enough to "see" it and to draw upon its energy. What he called upon us to "see" was how the whole world and every single person is a reflection of God. Everything, everyone is in God and God is in everything and everyone. Theologians today refer to this as *panentheism*. What a different world this would be if everyone had this insight! It is this insight that gives meaning to Jesus' whole life, to his acceptance of every type of person, sinner, child, leper. Everyone was valued.

John's Gospel, written with hindsight, could say: "To all who accepted him he gave the power to become children of God" (1:12). The basis of John's sense of the new Kingdom is the new body of people who will put their trust in God, and do the things that Jesus was doing. They were to be action people, doing things together, spiritually united. Jesus does not simply preach about God, but preaches God-in-action, with and within humanity.

But Jesus was more than simply an example to us, giving us a model of how to live. By his life, death, and rising to a higher form of life he empowered the whole of humankind to make the necessary breakthrough from our present powerlessness and assume the power of daughters and sons of God: to live a life in awareness of and governed by an entirely new humanity-God relationship, consequent upon which is a new person-to-person relationship. (We will come back to how Jesus empowers us in the chapter on *An Empowered Person*.)

The Church's perennial task is to focus the Good News of the gospel in a manner and in terms that are meaningful to each age. The Good News is not a series of disconnected doctrines. It is a single coherent message about the God-human relationship. Recall the words of Dietrich Bonhoeffer: "Jesus calls men, not to a new religion, but to life."

The focus of the Church's presentation can change and must change from age to age and from culture to culture, under the guidance of the Spirit. While not denying the value of other focuses from past periods of the Church's history, we are concerned today with that focus which holds increasing meaning for us in recent decades. The focus is returning to Jesus' original announcement of the Kingdom with all its implications. The Church is the community that gives witness to the world of what humanity is destined to become, because the Church itself has become fully conscious of the world's destiny. That, at least, is the theory!

The Kingdom, being greater than the Church, is brought about by all people of good will, some of whom will be Church members, the majority will not. These promoters of the Kingdom are the new

People of God of our New Testament times. "Not everyone who calls me 'Lord, Lord' will enter the Kingdom of heaven, but only those who do what my Father in heaven wants them to do" (Matthew 7:21).

Future times must be marked by a change in orientation from a Church which is over against the world, drawing people into its membership for their salvation, to a Church which sees itself as an instrument of change within society. From a Church which understood its mission to be that of attracting people to itself, to a Church with a mission to go out and evangelize human culture and values, transforming humanity from within and making it new.

To follow Jesus' injunction: "Set your hearts on God's Kingdom first, and his justice and all the rest will be given to you" (Matthew 6.33) means not only giving the Kingdom primacy but in its primacy the Kingdom makes everything else relative. The Church is relative to the Kingdom. Followed logically, this means that wherever the Church places itself above the Kingdom, or in any way gives a sign in contradiction to the Kingdom, the Church has lost its *raison d'etre*. The Church, as the Christian community, is present to give a witness to Kingdom-living which means it will always be a minority community in the world: the leaven, and no more. Its mission, like that of Jesus, is to manifest the Reign of God, not to gather as many people as possible into its membership.

Wherever in the world we see actions bringing about healing, liberating, reconciling, uniting, and good news being given to the poor (Luke 4:16-21), there we see the Kingdom blossoming. It may be happening within the Church or outside the Church and even despite the Church.

In summary, we can say:

- The main recorded example and teaching of Jesus is about living as a "Kingdom of God person," that is by recognizing the presence of the Divine in everyone.
- The Christian Church and individual Christians should be promoting Kingdom values, not Church doctrine or

membership. This will be done mostly in areas of life totally unconnected with the Church.

- The new awareness of our day is about recognizing these possibilities and encouraging the development of Kingdom values to transform society.

matters for pondering or discussion

1. In your experience, what are the factors that hold Churches back from witnessing and promoting the values of the Kingdom?

2. Some current theologians argue that the time of institutional religion is coming to an end and that a much broader and wider spirituality will take its place. What are your views on this?

3. If you attend a church, what would you want to say to your church leaders about this Kingdom orientation?

4. If your standpoint is outside the Church, how do you view institutional religion?

three

a universe person …

… regards the Universe as God's primary revelation.

The context of our lives is infinitely larger – spatially infinitely larger – than that in which Church doctrines and Church structures were formed. When the prayer was composed for imposing ashes on the foreheads of Christians on Ash Wednesday – "Remember, you are dust and to dust you will return" – the dust referred to was the dust of the disintegrated body in the coffin. Today, those same words, with a slight adjustment, have a different meaning, reminding us that we are the fall-out of the stars: "Remember, you are stardust and to stardust you will return." Dom Bede Griffiths, the Benedictine monk, wrote to a friend from his ashram in India: "The elements which make up the human body, and therefore the body of Jesus in his mother's womb, were being prepared when the original explosion of the matter of the Universe took place."

The world that Jesus knew and spoke about was bounded in the West by the Mediterranean Sea and in the North by the Alps, although his Greek contemporaries had already determined the circumference and radius of the Earth and had even calculated the distance from the Earth to the Moon. Furthermore, Jesus' Earth was the shape of a saucer with water all around the rim, with Heaven above the clouds and Sheol below. When St Paul wrote to the Roman Christians: "Ever since God created the world, his invisible qualities, both his eternal power and his divine nature, have been clearly seen; they are perceived in the things God has made" (1:20), he had no idea that the Universe had come into being some fifteen billion years previously and that over the last 600 million years there had been 22 known partial extinctions of Earth's species, and one major extinction 220 million years ago in which it is estimated that 90% of species vanished. Nor of course did he have any idea that human beings arrived on Earth in only the last few minutes, so to speak. Then when he wrote his second letter to the Christians in Corinth (which we know as First Corinthians) he thought the world was to end in his lifetime (1 Cor.7:31; 10:11).

Learning of the vastness of the Universe, with its ten billion galaxies, of which our Milky Way with its ten billion stars is only one, we now have a different concept of our place in creation. No longer can we regard ourselves as special. The original act of creation – if we can so name the Big Bang – and all the events and physical formations and millions of different species of plant and animal were not simply a run-up to produce the human species, as if we humans were really what the Creator was planning for all the time! Such a human-centered view, still held by some and found in Church writing, is no longer tenable. True, we humans, on this planet at least, are the only creatures able to think about ourselves thinking. True, we are the last – and very late – arrivals, but we can no longer be certain that we are the final product. We measure our human age in only thousands of years as against the billions of the Universe history. Distinguished scientists, like Martin Rees, the Astronomer Royal, believe that we are approaching the limit of understanding: the very vastness of the cosmos, of which 95% is Dark Matter, and the complexities of organisms, might now seem to lie forever beyond the limitations of our minds. We are very puny!

Our lives are being continually affected, not only by the forces around us, but by great shifts of energy on a cosmic scale. John Archibald Wheeler, the theoretical physicist who worked on the search for a Unified Field Theory, says: "The Universe does not exist 'out there,' independent of us. We are inescapably involved in bringing about that which appears to be happening. We are not simply observers. We are participants. In some strange sense this is a participatory Universe."

"Creation" is still a word widely used to speak about the coming about of the Universe. This word would better be replaced by "origin" when speaking of the Big Bang, while "creation" will increasingly take on the meaning of the moment-by-moment continuance of existence of everything. God did not "create" as an original act, and there it all was – at least in potential. Creation is the continuing activity of the timeless Divine energy operating in the eternal NOW.

The very meaning of "world" is changing its currency. In Scripture it is often used to speak of the whole Universe. "It is by faith that we understand that the world was created by one word from God" (Hebrews 11:3). "God loved the world so much that he gave his only Son ..." (John 3:16). In this latter case "the world" refers to the world of humanity, as distinct from Planet Earth; the sense in which we use the word today. John's Gospel recounts Jesus using "world" in a gnostic sense of being evil in contrast with the spiritual that is good. Jesus prayed to his Father: "I do not ask you to take them out of the world, but I do ask you to keep them safe from the Evil One. Just as I do not belong to the world, they do not belong to the world" (John 17:15-16). Thus is associated "the world, the flesh and the devil" as in a Collect for Morning Prayer in the Book of Common Prayer.

By contrast, Eastern mystics refer to the whole of creation as "the body of God." As our bodies manifest our person, so creation manifests God. The eastern religions go so far as to say that the whole of creation is God: God is the whole of creation. We call this *pantheism*. The great religions of the West, however, maintain a distinction between the Creator and creation. To speak of God being all-pervasive in the Universe, is not to say that God equals Universe.

There is no Divine truth that reaches us from anywhere outside the Universe. We have to discover Truth, about God and God's purpose for creation, from within creation itself. Thomas Berry, the cultural historian and theologian, has said: "The Universe is the primary revelation of the Divine, the primary scripture, the primary locus of divine-human communion."

matters for pondering or discussion

1. Has it been your belief that God created the whole Universe as a prelude to creating human beings?

2. The Church describes each human person as being directly created by God, or, in the words of the Second Vatican Council: "The only creature on Earth which God willed for itself." What are your thoughts about this?

3. Are we human beings the most important species to God? Why?

4. Can we today ignore the theory of evolution, including our own evolution?

5. Do you think of God as within the Universe or outside, beyond the Universe?

four

an ecologically-aware person ...

... does not consider oneself superior to the rest of creation.

ew of us today would not claim to be ecologically aware. We recycle our bottles, tins, and newspapers. We save energy by switching off unnecessary lights (sometimes!). We cannot avoid hearing about the impending disaster for our planet on account of the depletion of the ozone layer and the climatic change that results. Yes, we are aware. We are even concerned. Concerned enough, maybe, to voice our support for wind turbines and for means of energy creation other than by using up dwindling stocks of fossil fuels. We campaign for sustainable energy production.

At another level, we may be vociferous for animal rights, condemning fox hunting and all scientific experimentation on animals.

This level of ecological awareness is increasing, especially among younger people with their concern for the well-being of the whole planet. But this concern operates, nevertheless, within the traditional Hebraic-Christian paradigm that places the human being at the peak of the creation pyramid. Our Scripture (the Book of Genesis) tells us we are in charge. We claim to be created in the image of God. If we think of God as above, outside creation, then we too are, in our own respect, "above" the rest of creation. Our use of the word "supernatural" says it all! All the lower levels are there for our use and pleasure. We can treat them accordingly. We mostly mistreat them accordingly. We depend upon the Earth, but does the Earth depend on us?

The word "ecology" comes from the Greek word *oikos* meaning "household." We consider ourselves to be householders of our planet. Did God not say in the act of creation: "Now we will make human beings in our own image, in the likeness of ourselves. They will have *power* over the fish, the birds of heaven, the cattle, all wild beasts and all the reptiles that crawl upon the earth"? At least this is what we read in the Book of Genesis (1:26). And once created, Adam and Eve were told: "Be fruitful, multiply, fill the Earth and *conquer* it" (1:28). Today we still speak of conquering nature, as if we owned it and had to tame it to serve us. Our society is still, as it was when the words of the Book of Genesis were written only a few centuries before the Jesus event, living with the structure of a hierarchical society in which people and objects are given value according to the use they are to society.

Today's concern for the well-being of creation is skin-deep only. The Norwegian philosopher Arne Naess calls this ecological paradigm "shallow ecology." There is an alternative paradigm, "deep ecology," and this is the way in which tomorrow's Christian relates to creation. The two are based on different theological perspectives. The former, we have seen, is that of humanity considering itself superior to the rest of creation – that we are the ultimate product. Deep ecology, on the other hand, has us see ourselves as part of the total natural environment. If we continue to think in terms of a First Cause, that which caused the singularity we name the "Big Bang," then we will name that First cause "God." In which case there is no other image in creation than that of God. It is the Divine energy that sustains everything. We are, in the most literal sense, made from Divine Energy. There is no other source. Everything bears the Divine imprint. Meister Eckhart, the medieval mystic, expresses this beautifully: "Every creature is a word of God and a book about God." In this perspective, all living things, all the non-living things too, have the same intrinsic value: a Divine value. All are willed by the Creator. All have a part to play. Tomorrow's Christians are more aware than previous generations that every creature has its own intrinsic value. Albert Schweitzer wrote:

The purpose of nature, with her thousands of appearances of life, is not understood as merely the presupposition of man's existence ... and humanity may not conceive of itself as the purpose of the infinite world.

We are helped in this understanding today by the insights of quantum physics, which reveal how everything in nature is fundamentally interconnected and interdependent. Without knowing anything of quantum physics, however, the poet Francis Thompson wrote, in *The Mistress of Vision*:

> All things by immortal power
> Near and far,
> Hiddenly to each other linked are,
> That thou canst not stir a flower
> Without trembling of a star.

Our learning that we share 98.5% of our DNA with chimpanzees makes us more aware how closely we as human beings are related to the animal world and our responsibility for it.

Shallow ecology can be called a materialist's view of nature, valuing it by what is useful, while deep ecology can be said to be a spiritual vision. We find this latter vision among the Aborigines, the North American Indians, the Celts, among all pre-technological people who do not make the distinction we in the West make between the sacred and the profane. They had a deep reverence for Spirit dwelling in and energizing everything. They were able to recognize that everything, but everything, contains a spark of the Divine.

matters for pondering or discussion

1. Do you find it hard to think of your pets as "made in the image of God"?

2. Would you agree that the paradigm of shallow ecology corresponds with our belief in a theistic God "out there," and deep ecology with our belief in an immanent God?

3. Can you think of any other species that treats its own members with the amount of violence with which we humans treat each other?

4. If you are a vegetarian or a vegan, what reasons do you give to people for your choice of lifestyle?

5. It is calculated that if all six billion of us on this planet were to live with our western lifestyle, we would need nine planets to support us. Are you prepared to live more simply?

five

a global person ...

... rejoices in the diversity of the human family.

"Globalization" is a constantly recurring word these days to describe the process whereby individuals, groups, and countries are becoming increasingly inter-related. The word is used differently according to one's concerns.

Through the eyes of commerce, globalization means the growth of the transnational corporations – Nike, Coca-Cola, McDonald's, Exxon, Mobil, General Motors, for example – each having revenues greater than the combined economic output (GDP) of the forty-eight least developed countries. Aided by the treaties of the World Trade Organization, they are intent upon gaining still more power and control.

Then there is the increasing networking of information worldwide. Microsoft, AOL, Yahoo, Vodaphone have become household names. In 1930 a three-minute trans-Atlantic telephone call cost over 100 dollars in today's value, while now it costs just 27 cents. Only a few decades ago, to obtain information on a particular subject might have meant traveling to a specialized library, in another country even. Today, with the World Wide Web, information about almost any subject, anywhere in the world, is instantly obtainable by everyone on a home computer. And the processing power of computers is increasing at a rate of 35% a year.

The globalization of culture is another aspect of our shrinking world. We travel more to visit peoples of other cultures. World tourism counted 260 million visitors in 1980 and 590 million in 1998 and is expected to rise to 1.6 billion by 2020. But we do not even have to travel. We now meet other cultures in our home towns, if not in person then in the plethora of ethnic restaurants. Increasing international migration means greater cultural contact between countries and people. A trip down the fruit and vegetable aisle in our local supermarket is a tour of the Third World. Ideas, goods, people, and money travel more, faster, more cheaply, and in greater quantities than ever before. We live within a tapestry of cultures. Like it or not, it is now generally accepted that globalization is an unstoppable force.

Through electronic banking between the globe's Stock Exchanges, speculators gamble 1.5 trillion dollars each day. This too is "globalization"! The IMF (International Monetary Fund) stated in May 1997: "Globalization refers to the growing interdependencies of countries worldwide through the increasing volume and variety of cross-border transactions in goods and services, and of international capital flows; and also through the rapid and widespread diffusion of all kinds of technology."

This is a very materialist definition. Fortunately a more human perspective was given at the Millennium Summit in September 2000 when the United Nations played host to the largest ever gathering of world leaders. Their Declaration states: "We believe that the central challenge we face today is to ensure that globalization becomes a positive force for all the world's people."

Can we see any connection between our increasing globalization as described above and God's design for us earthlings that Jesus proclaimed in the metaphor of the Kingdom of God?

Can we recognize in any aspects of today's globalization a movement toward the fulfillment of that unity for which Jesus prayed?

We might recognize a number of features of globalization as being indicative of an increasing unity of humanity coming about.

At the level of religions, the features of globalization that

I mentioned above are causing us to become more aware of the richness and holiness of the followers of Eastern faiths – Hinduism, Buddhism, Sikhism – who now live among us. Through the recent opening up of dialogue, we are more aware of how their particular insights into the spiritual journey can enrich our own understanding of Christian revelation.

The phenomenon of globalization marks the end of the supremacy of the Christian West. Culturally, Christianity has always been western and western culture over the last two millennia has been Christian. The certainties that underpinned western society, that gave it the moral right to attempt to colonize the rest of the world, derived from belief in the unchangeable values of the Bible. But such cultural Christianity is at an end.

Over the last decades there has been a shift of the center of gravity of Christians of all Churches from the Northern to the Southern hemisphere. The Church will become a Church of the developing nations, no longer of the rich nations. It will, like the early Church, be a Church of the poor, the powerless, not seeking security in alliances with governments and big business. It will be a non-clerical Church with increased lay participation and co-responsibility, taking its shape from the ordinary people. It will be de-centralized, not seeking uniformity, more open to other cultures, other Churches, other faiths. It will express itself less in order, legislation, organization; it will put more trust in relationships than in efficiency. In a word, the Church of the future will be more gospel-like.

The World Wide Web, another contributor to globalization, is unwittingly militating against the hierarchical structures of society and of our institutions. It is a great equalizer, ignoring time and distance. Anyone, anywhere, with no need to advertise their "authority" can post their point of view on everyone else's screen. There is no controlling parent figure, ecclesiastical or otherwise, to censor or disapprove. By networking power is exercised horizontally. This is the new force shaping world opinion and bringing about change. This dissolving of vertical hierarchical power is in keeping with the vision Jesus had for our mutual relationships as sisters and brothers with a common Father. This was his vision of the Kingdom society that he not only announced through what he said but demonstrated by his own relationships with people (Matthew 22:2-10; 23:6-10; Mark 10:13-16, 42-45; 12:14; John 13:4-15).

Today's Christians' concerns have become planetary. We have a concern for injustices practiced in far-off countries, for the mass poverty in the Southern hemisphere, for the suffering caused by natural disasters at the other side of the globe. We now feel personally concerned about these as never before.

We are alarmed at the environmental effect on the whole of our planet by our misuse and plundering of the Earth's natural resources.

We have set up an International Court of Justice to ensure justice and the rule of law in international affairs.

The problems of refugees and asylum-seekers have become our own problems and it is on a world scale that we are challenged by the widening gap between the rich and the poor, of which, incidentally, one of the causes is economic globalization.

All these concerns reflect Kingdom values.

While most of us became aware of the phenomenon of globalization only in the past two decades, Teilhard de Chardin was writing about it more than sixty years ago. He usually referred to it as "planetization" or sometimes as "hominization of the planet." He wrote: "No evolutionary future awaits human beings except in association with all other human beings." He foresaw our future as a new level of (world-wide) human society – the super-society – which would experience an even higher level of consciousness, a corporate or global consciousness. This is not just a sociological feature. It is a spiritual matter. At least it is if we are able to recognize what is happening in our world as a great move forward toward that unity for which Jesus prayed.

matters for pondering or discussion

1. There are many groups that demonstrate against globalization. Do you think this cause should be supported or not?

2. When you buy food, do you consciously make a choice for those goods originating in the poorer countries?

3. Do you buy, or even sell, Fair Trade goods?

4. Which of the Overseas Aid Agencies do you support?

5. How would you argue for the right of refugees to be housed in your road?

6. Does globalization make people feel that they have less control over their future? If so, why?

six

an evolving person ...

... believes our understanding of Divine truths also evolves.

In eastern and western philosophies, and in the great religions of the world, it has been traditionally assumed that a cause is greater than that which it causes. The higher, greater spiritual realms cause the creation of matter, which belongs to the lower realms of existence. Now, in the West, modern science reverses the order, understanding creation as proceeding from below upwards, from the simple to the complex. We call this process "evolution."

The Universe is evolving, we are told. We human beings are part of the evolving process. Of all the features composing our worldview today, features that are causing Christians to re-think their beliefs, I suggest the predominant factor – in the sense of affecting so many others – is precisely our present understanding of evolution. Whether or not we accept the manner of its happening as proposed by Darwin – due to the survival of the fittest – the fact of the evolution of our species is now more than a hypothesis. It has caused our worldview to change from the static to the dynamic. Everything is continually in a process of change. Ideas, theories, and doctrines, and beliefs too, are in constant process of change, their statements no longer considered as set in concrete for all time.

Further, we have to acknowledge that change is happening at an increasing speed. Witness the growing gap in the outlook on life between teenagers and their parents today. In the fields of electronics, genetic engineering, global marketing, changes are happening ever more rapidly.

To think of change as evolution is not to make a value judgement about it. It is not to say that life is getting better, if by better we mean more fulfilling. Who is to say that the home with every conceivable labor-saving gadget and physical comfort makes its owners more happy than are the peasant farmers in the village in Zambia where I used to live, whose lives were extremely simple by our standards, but by that very fact had few financial and material worries.

We live in an evolving Universe, journeying from the Big Bang to the Big Crunch or the Big Stretch or whatever. There is no escape from that. But as the only creatures on this planet who have a free will, we alone are able to make choices. We can choose whether to go along with change or whether to oppose it. We can decide which new things are for our good and which are detrimental. The Christian has a measure with which to make personal judgments as to which path to take.

The Christian sees the whole evolving process in the light of a belief that God is bringing about His purposes. St Paul recognized that we are on a journey toward our final fulfillment in union with God and recognized too that it was a painful journey:

> I consider that what we suffer at this present time cannot be
> compared at all with the glory that is going to be revealed to
> us. All of creation waits with eager longing for God to reveal
> his children ... [there is] the hope that creation itself would
> one day be set free from its slavery to decay and would
> share the glorious freedom of the children of God. For we
> know that up to the present time all of creation groans with
> pain, like the pain of childbirth. (Romans 8:18-22)

As we move forward, tomorrow's Christians will, as mature adults, have to face up to the number of disjunctions we are already experiencing between what is proposed for our religious belief and our day-to-day experience of life. Some of these we will be looking at in the chapters that follow.

Are we to continue to believe, for instance, that the human being is the only creature on Earth directly created by God, the only creature wanted for itself? Are we to believe that the millions of other creatures, most of which have already vanished from our planet, were simply a preparation for the creation of human beings?

Are we still to do our God-thinking with the cosmological view of the world that the Israelites had 2,000 years ago, as we read it in the Bible, when today's astrophysicists explore the immensity of the Universe way beyond our imagining? Are we still to raise our eyes to Heaven, a place where God is, in making our prayers, and to continue to speak of Jesus "coming down to Earth" and "ascending" back to his Father? Do we still think of Heaven and Hell as actual places rather than modes of being and relating, life in another dimension of energy?

The theory of evolution makes us re-think the biblical account of a once-perfect world, a Garden of Eden, of us all as descended from a single pair of human beings directly created by God, and of a "Fall"' from such a state. And with this adjustment of our ideas, what are we to make of the need for Redemption from a fallen state, of God requiring His son to become a blood sacrifice of appeasement? (We shall consider this in a future chapter.)

Today young people require authenticity. They are prepared to take on board beliefs that make sense to their experience of life. "Be real!" What is proposed to them must relate to their experience. This is what gives it and its proposers authenticity.

Our theology is evolving. Not because the Church is receiving new revelations but because we are continually probing deeper into the truths we possess, seeing them in a new light, a light thrown from our increased knowledge and understanding of our world. God, however, does not evolve. God is always in the timeless, eternal NOW. It is we who are evolving in our consciousness, in our understanding of our relationship to the historical and physical totality of creation. And in consequence we are continually evolving in the manner in which we relate to God.

Jesus too was a feature of evolution. Why this Divine visitation only after some half a million years of humans inhabiting the world? I believe that it could only happen when human consciousness had developed to the point where the message he brought could be understood. Not only had humanity to evolve to that point, but such a person as Jesus, as one sharing our full humanity, could not have emerged in earlier centuries. He himself, with his higher consciousness, was a product of the evolutionary process.

Tomorrow's Christians are more aware of the implications of evolution for their faith. More aware of the need to re-express our Christian beliefs in terms of today's knowledge. They are more aware that we are called to partner God as co-creators, to point our human evolution in the direction to which we understand humanity to be called.

matters for pondering or discussion

1. List some of the major changes that have happened in your lifetime which have caused you to re-think your Christian beliefs.

2. The Creationists believe literally in the creation story as told in the Book of Genesis. What persuades you otherwise?

3. Is there a fundamental question with which you would challenge this or that change in society to help you to decide whether to go along with it or to oppose it?

4. It is suggested that Jesus made his appearance only when human consciousness was able to comprehend his message and take his Good News to heart. Do you see any signs that humanity has changed for the better over the two thousand years since then?

5. Why does our evolution have to be the painful process that St Paul understands it to be?

seven

a non-theistic person ...

... is shifting from a perception of an external God to an all-pervading God.

It is hard to imagine anyone, calling themselves a Christian, declaring that they had no relationship with God! Yet two books, each by a respected theologian, have been published recently with surprising titles: *Christianity without God* and *Religion without God*. Neither of them is denying the existence of God. They are making the point that the traditional – and current – way in which God is described or thought about is no longer speaking to the majority of people in the West today.

In 1998 when Tony Bullimore's yacht capsized in a world race, he thought he was about to die. Afterwards he was quoted by a newspaper as saying: "There was nothing more I could do alone. I needed help: I started to pray. I have prayed only two or three times in my life but I tried to get through to God through an intense concentration of thought." I describe his kind of God as the "fire-extinguisher God": to be left quietly in the corner, hidden from sight if possible, but pulled out and relied upon in emergencies, when the situation gets beyond our human ability to cope.

What I call the traditional ideas of God are expressed in a number of different ways. There is the God who can do anything: prevent earthquakes, control the weather (how many prayers are offered on this subject, many quite contrary?!), prevent the Holocaust. Why doesn't He? A God who is on our side in war, who sits in a cosmic phone box to answer every call. A God who requires praise and gratitude but who rules by fear, the book-keeper of our good and evil deeds who dispenses post-mortem rewards and punishments. He is a loving Father but nevertheless required Abraham to kill his only son and sent His own son, Jesus, down to Earth to suffer the most appalling sacrificial death in order that He might be avenged for the sinfulness of humanity.

Is this a parody? Then look again at the hymns we sing and the prayers we say in church. Our theologians may be presenting a different understanding but the official worshipping Church retains and enforces the imagery of a past age – an imagery it is hard to escape from.

I believe there are five areas of unease about God today, which are causing us to look afresh at that mystery that cannot be contained by words.

First, there is the image of God as the supplier of our needs. The God who is "up there," whose job is to look after us, indeed to serve us. Not only to ensure that our lives are comfortable – as Jonah expected (4:5-6) – but to answer our every demand and to be life's safety net. Secondly, there is the God who is kept in a separate box from the rest of life. In the West we compartmentalize life into the sacred and the secular, the holy and the profane, the spiritual and the material. Sunday is God's day: the rest of the week we get on with living.

Thirdly, the image of a God to be feared is deep within the consciousness of many Christians. He is the law-giver, the judge, the punisher. This is God the policemen. Fourthly, there is the God who is outside and "above" creation. How many of us still point upwards to indicate the deity? We are made in the image of God, we are told, so we believe ourselves to be at the pinnacle of creation, exercising our god-power over every other species on the planet.

These are concepts of a God – a male God – made to our own image and likeness. A God who thinks and acts as we do. They are not helpful in the context of our present-day world.

Today, for many, the concept is of a God who grows smaller with every advance of science, only there to fill the gaps which science cannot explain; the God who is gradually being pushed to the margins as we human beings "play god" with our ever-increasing abilities: from the ability to design our children to the ability to annihilate our entire planet by a nuclear explosion.

Bishop John Spong defines the theistic God as: "A being supernatural in power, dwelling outside this world and invading the world periodically to accomplish the divine will." He goes on to say: "God, understood theistically, is thus quite clearly a human construct. Theism is not the same as God."

We must start our considerations then from the premise that "God" is the name we give to the Reality that cannot be named. We cannot know God neat. We can only build up a picture of God from what we think of as His attributes. And these are simply a magnification to the "nth" degree of the human qualities we admire in ourselves. Because we value Life, Love, Truth, Goodness, Beauty, Justice, and Freedom – and many more – we conceive of God as the one who possesses all these to an infinite degree. So our image of God is of a Super-human. We can do no other as human beings than think humanly of God in human terms. The German theologian, Karl Barth (1886-1968) reminds us: "God is God, not man writ large."

The very first image of God we built up as children, and consequently the way we related to God in childhood, came from human sources. Chiefly from our relationship with our parents and to a lesser degree from our relationship with other significant persons or groups. These relationships were the foundation of our self-esteem, our ability to appreciate ourselves, and so our ability to relate to the God whom we learnt about through instruction and whose presence we experienced through our religious practice: our prayer, worship, Bible stories, the natural world, and more. Whatever our head tells us about God today, it is very difficult to delete those deep-down first childhood images. And yet we are required to grow in our adult relationship with God as in all other relationships.

The study of different cultures in our present world reveals that there are many differing, even contradictory, concepts of God abroad. We even see how a development took place among the Jewish people in the pages of the Hebrew Bible (the Christian's "Old Testament"). From a belief (in Abraham's time) that each tribe had its own god, then to an appreciation that the Hebrew God was the greatest God, then, after their Exile, that there was only one God. The early Christians, studying the words of Jesus, took the concept further and understood that there were three different expressions of the Divine which they named Father, Son, and Spirit.

The Hindus speak of God manifest and God unmanifest, which is equivalent to our speaking of God immanent and God transcendent. The Middle Ages mystic Meister Eckhart similarly distinguished between God and the Godhead. The latter in each expression is, in the words of the theologian Paul Tillich "the God beyond God," the Ultimate Reality beyond our human knowing. Whereas the former is God "brought down to our size," the God we can imagine and speak about, pray to, have a relationship with. It is our way of perceiving this human-relating God with which contemporary people are attempting to grapple. God is not a human invention, but our formulas for God are. Wordsworth recognized that it is the essence of the God instinct that matters, not the explanation.

Instead of starting from a pre-conceived idea of God and working downwards from that, so to speak (God is the supreme expression of energy, God is the Ground of all Being, God is the Reality that underlies our ultimate concerns), we have to start from the bottom upwards, from our human experience: the supreme expression of energy, we call God; the Ground of all Being, we call God; that reality that underlies our ultimate concerns, we call God. Our experience of Love, we call God. Our experience of Being, we call God.

We can experience God but we cannot know God. We can only know our own experience of God and the description of other people's experience of God. What Jesus said about God was not the last word. It was his experience within the background of his culture and times.

God is not a being, as against other beings, nor the Supreme

Being. God is Being: a verb not a noun. And we consciously partake in the Being. Each of us is a human expression of Being: a human Being.

matters for pondering or discussion

1. What image of God is revealed by the way you pray?

2. Are you afraid of God?

3. How do you view creation and God's activity in it?

4. Do you feel challenged by any of the ideas in this chapter? If so, which?

5. How would you speak of your perception of God to a life-long non-believer?

6. What would you answer the questioner in the street who asks you: "Do you believe in a personal God?"

7. Is there a conflict between the "God within" and "God the creator of the Universe"? Is one a small God and one a big God?

eight

a co-creating person ...

... lives life in partnership with God.

Our role as human beings, as the only self-aware species on this Earth, is to be partners with the Creator in bringing about the kind of world that God wishes this to be. This applies to everyone but to Christians especially because we are, in the words of a World Council of Churches document: "that segment of the world which reveals the final goal towards which God is working for the whole world."

To recognize our role as co-creators does not infer that we and God are equal partners. The totality of creating energy has its source in God. We partner God in that we use that energy within the dimension of time-space to bring about the kind of world God wishes this to be. It is to acknowledge that creation was not a once-and-for-all act at the "beginning of time" – which we associate with the Big Bang some 15 billion years ago – but is an ongoing process not yet complete. Our co-operation is in giving form to, or material-izing, God's creative energy.

Further, it is to acknowledge that creation is in process of evolving from nothingness to completion. In its incompleteness we can recognize the suffering entailed in its evolving journey. In a previous chapter we saw that St Paul recognized this. Suffering, and even evil, are a consequence of the incompleteness of creation. Evil, for which human beings alone are responsible, comes about because of our pursuing the wrong paths in an attempt to satisfy our needs. So the central battle of life is not between good and evil, as it has been presented in ancient cultures – and still too often in the Church – but the central drama in which each of us is intimately involved is the process of an evolving creation. Consequently the ultimate goal is not the victory over evil by good but the completion of God's design for creation.

In the realm of the eternal NOW, it is already present, but within created time it is still in process. The length of time it will take until fulfillment is dependent upon our human co-operation with the process.

In terms of the personal life of each of us, our "work" on Earth is not the salvation of our souls, but our engagement in the process of creation. This is an exciting task because it leads inevitably to the fulfillment of the Divine intention, whereas a life spent in concern for personal salvation can occasion worries and doubts, neurosis and despair.

In current discussions about euthanasia or about recent advances in our scientific knowledge and the use to which we put them, for example in experimenting with genetically modified food, in cloning animals and even human beings, and in all our attempts to have greater control over the laws of nature so as to bend them to our benefit, we often hear people giving a warning with the words: "We are playing God." The warning is given as if there was a department of life that God allows us to play with but that there are frontiers beyond which is God's area of control. But who is to say where that frontier lies? Such warnings assume a God who would rather we were not creators, despite His having given us the intelligence so to act. Are we not so ready to declare that we are "made in the image of God"? But God is a creating God!

We took a giant step over the frontier when, on 6 August 1945, we wrested control from God of the very existence of our planet. It was the day we dropped the first atomic bomb when war-making shifted from genocide to omnicide. By allowing this planet to continue to exist, despite the nuclear arsenal humanity still holds and which could destroy it several times over, we have seized from "the Almighty" the mastery over life on Earth. But further, with our adventures into the field of genetic engineering, we have given ourselves the power to re-shape all life forms. We have really taken "creation" into our own hands. It makes all our former attempts at "playing God" look puny!

What counts is not what we are able to do but what we do with our ability to do it. If as Christians we take love as the supreme law of life, then we have to apply that criterion to our new technologies. Are they making us a more loving united people – or the contrary?

matters for pondering or discussion

1. Would you regard energy, in all its forms – from physical force at one end of the scale to love at the other – as a manifestation of God?

2. What are the grounds for Christians claiming to have the clearest knowledge of the purpose of the Universe?

3. Does our partnership with God as co-creators stretch beyond Planet Earth?

4. Human beings are very recent arrivals indeed upon this planet. Is it presumptuous to think of God requiring our co-operation?

nine

a balanced person ...

... gives equal attention to body, mind, and spirit.

"**O**f which should you take more care, your body or your soul?" was the catechism question I learned in my tender years. And of course the answer was the soul because the soul is immortal.

In Greek philosophy, however, and in the early Christian writers, as in the Indian tradition, we find a threefold distinction made: spirit, soul, and body. St Paul speaks of: "... your whole being, spirit, soul and body ..." (1 Thessalonians 5:23). In New Testament Greek we have *pneuma* (spirit, the supra-personal, the Divine Spirit, manifesting itself in and through a person), *psyche* (soul or mind which belongs to the person). Thus we can speak of "my soul" but not "my spirit." We can only say, as St Paul does, "the Spirit is in me." Thirdly, *soma* (the body, material being). The brain is *soma* but our thoughts, feelings, consciousness, memory, our mind are *psyche*.

Gradually this tripartite division or aspect of the human person shrank into a twofold division: spirit and nature or mind and matter or soul and body.

In the catechism approach there lingers still the ghost of Gnosticism, which featured widely in the early centuries of the Church. Namely, that the soul and all matters spiritual were good but that all natural matter, the body for instance, was tainted with evil. Consequently it was the soul which was all-important and all else was only a means to enable the soul to be "saved," to be released from its bondage in matter. The Church eventually declared Gnosticism to be a heresy.

With primacy being given to the soul, our life on Earth came to be considered as simply a preparation for "the next life." Consequently all of nature was regarded as no more than a means to an end: there to be used by human beings for easing their passage to everlasting life. This is illustrated by a remark made by a Christian fundamentalist, James Gaius Watt, Ronald Reagan's Secretary of the Interior: "The Earth [is] merely a temporary way station on the road to eternal life. It is unimportant except as a place of testing to get into Heaven." This is the same attitude to life on Earth as held by Muslim suicide bombers.

But today in the secular world we have returned to a tripartite distinction of body, mind, and spirit. In our cities New Age organizations hold "Body, Mind, and Spirit" exhibitions in which the "spirit" element covers a wide variety of interests from healing one's aura to T'ai-chi, to meditation, to crystals and lots more. "Spirit" in this context is more akin to soul *psyche* than to the presence of the Divine Spirit *pneuma*.

What we notice in the world at large today is that whereas a great deal of time and energy is spent on furthering the body (gyms, health foods, jogging) and the mind (further education, University of the Third Age), less concern is being given to our spiritual development.

We are like a three-legged stool. Unless all three legs are of equal length the stool is useless. Each of the three dimensions of our lives contributes to the other two. We are only too aware how mental stress can induce physical sickness. We are all of a piece. To be bodily, mentally, and spiritually healthy tomorrow's Christian ensures that all three are kept in balance. Over-emphasis of one impairs the effectiveness of the others.

Many Christians follow the traditional practice of doing some form of penance or mortification during the Lenten season in preparation for Easter. Their intentions and practices vary. Some fast or abstain from certain foods. In our childhood a favorite (at least for adults to impose upon us!) was to "give up sweets for Lent."

Tomorrow's Christian understands that since God is not a person whose good or bad opinion of us can be influenced by what we do, not loving us less nor loving us more, the value of, say fasting, lies not only in strengthening our self-discipline, but in the good it does to our health, to our whole person. If whatever "penance" we undertake is not simply done to be something unpleasant for its own sake, but makes us more fit people in body, mind, and spirit, then this has a value. It enables us to be more like the person we were created to be. "We shall become more mature people, reaching to the very height of the Christ's full stature" (Ephesians 4:13).

matters for pondering or discussion

1. Do you have a sense of being able to please God by what you do?

2. What is your understanding of a "spiritual exercise"?

3. If you observe Lent, reflect upon the motive and value of your manner of observing it.

4. It is said in the West that we are a body that has a soul. In the East it is said that we are a soul that has a body. With which of these expressions do you feel more comfortable?

5. Does God love Mother Teresa as much as he loves Hitler?

ten

a right-brain person ...

... appreciates Wisdom, Intuition, Creativity.

Since the mid-1960s a variety of psychological studies have shown that our brains have a left and right hemisphere, each side specializing in different forms of activity. The left hemisphere analyses, discriminates, measures, names, and organizes. Its way of thinking is rational, lineal, going from A to B to C, from cause to effect. The right hemisphere sees in wholes, synthesizes, unites, detects patterns, comprehends the totality of A to Z. It is the creative, imaginative, intuitive part of the mind. The former is said to predominate in the masculine mind and the latter in the feminine.

Our western culture has, since the sixteenth and seventeenth centuries, favored rational knowledge over intuitive wisdom, science over religion, competition over co-operation, always enforced by our masculine-dominated society.

But for far longer the Church in the West has exercised a left-brain approach to religion. This is particularly apparent in the Church's attitude to belief and to worship. All other major religions are more concerned with the way in which their people live and relate than in what they believe. The beliefs of each are a means to an end; they are a help to living a more spiritual life. Christianity is an exception, in that what decides whether one can be called a Christian or not, whether one is in communion with the Church or not, is by presenting one with a statement of beliefs with the question: Do you accept these truths? Creeds appeared early in the Church's history in order to counteract heresy, the best known being the Nicene Creed of the year 325. We find the first mention of what is called the Apostles Creed around 380, while the much longer Athanasian Creed was drawn up sometime between 381 and 428. These were the ecclesiastical litmus tests to decide whether one was orthodox or heretical: whether one was "in" or "out." That this should be the approved criterion for deciding membership – and indeed one's salvation – is strange when considering that both Jesus and St Paul were much more concerned with how a follower should live than in what he or she believed.

Still today, the Creeds find a place in many forms of Church service. A Creed should have no place in worship. It is not a prayer. It belongs to the religious education class where its origins and content can be explained. It is a left-brain analytical treatment of Divine Truth. Doctrinal statements were agreed upon in order to bring about unity in the Christian community. Doctrine and structure are mutually reinforcing. If the doctrine is attacked the structure rescues it. If the structure is attacked the doctrine rescues it. For the Church to evolve, both doctrine and structure will have to change simultaneously.

Tomorrow's Christians realize that much of what they read in the Bible was written as an attempt to express an inexpressible mystery, an experience of what was believed to be Divine intervention, not meant to be a literal report of facts. They are descriptions written in a culture more open to wisdom than to rationalizing, to poetry than to facts. Examples of this are in the accounts of creation and the "Fall," the elements of the Christmas story and the Resurrection appearances.

If there is one word that describes the character of Church worship today it is the word "busy." The liturgy keeps the left-brain rational mind busy by being so wordy: the prayers, the hymns, the sermons, the Eucharistic rite, the exhortations. A call for "a few moments of silence" rarely lasts longer than a minute before the congregation starts fidgeting. People feel they must be continually active because they have come to church to do something for God!

Not so tomorrow's Christian, who is caught up in the contemporary attempt to recognize the values of the right brain: intuition, creativity, wisdom. This thrives on stillness, on silence, on awareness. Increasingly people today are turning to practices such as contemplative meditation, which opens the right brain, to what Buddhists call "mindfulness." For Christians such meditation is replacing "saying prayers." Today we witness an education policy increasingly geared to cultivate the creative, unifying, non-competitive potential of children. So many teachers and child-carers and parents remark to me that today's small children seem to be much more "aware," "connected," "intuitive" than ever they were at that age.

Unless the Church recognizes the current breakthrough to this new consciousness, to a greater left and right brain balance, and respects this in its forms of worship, people are going to be looking elsewhere than in their local church for their spiritual nourishment. Many are doing so already.

Tomorrow's Christians decide for themselves whether they consider themselves to be one with the Christian community, and it is not by a passive acceptance of the articles of a Creed or of definitions of doctrine. They are moving away from uniformity of belief to diversity in unity, upon the realization that Divine Truth can never be comprehensively encapsulated in a formula. What counts for them is how they experience God in the depth of their own lives, in their relationships with other people and as alive and active in creation. They then choose what is the most appropriate path for them to respond to this experience.

matters for pondering or discussion

1. Would you say you are predominantly a left-brain thinker or a right-brain thinker? How does this affect your spiritual life?

2. If you have anything to do with small children today, in nursery school, playgroup, or as parent or grandparent, have you yourself noticed what others are remarking upon, namely the presence of an inner wisdom less noticeable in previous generations?

3. What attempts are made in the liturgy and worship of your local church to help people benefit from moments of silence? Can you see a way of introducing or encouraging this?

4. Have you ever had explained to you the origin and reasons for drawing up the Creeds? Have you ever wondered why the Creeds go from the birth to the death of Jesus, omitting the very reason for his being among us: the proclamation of the Good News of what he called the Kingdom of God?

eleven

a sex-equality person ...

... challenges the influence of biblical patriarchy.

Tomorrow's Christian does not follow social fashion blindly but does believe that we have to look for signs of the presence and purpose of the Holy Spirit in the trends of contemporary society. This is what is meant by the World Council of Churches' statement: "It is the world that must be allowed to provide the agenda for the Churches." One trend becoming increasingly prominent is the role of women in society and consequently in the Church.

The values of the western world are more biblically formed than we often realize. And the Bible is both patriarchal and hierarchical. This is certainly true of the Hebrew Scriptures (the Christians' Old Testament) right from its first book and the story of the creation of Adam and Eve. What we have to remember is that this is not an historical account of events but a mythological explanation to convey theological beliefs, written only several hundred years before the Jesus event, when patriarchy and hierarchy were already the social pattern of Jewish life and so it was written in this context.

The effect has been that throughout history till now, women have been submerged in this scriptural tradition and sin has been located and symbolized in women: Eve the temptress.

Yet we read in the Book of Genesis: "God said: 'Now we will make human beings, they will be like us and resemble us' ... God created man in the image of himself, in the image of God he created him,

male and female he created them" (1:26-27). Obviously an image
of God in human form is not a mirror image. We human beings, as
indeed the whole of creation, can say that we are the image of God,
that we reflect God, in that the whole Universe is pervaded with
God's energy. Nothing exists without it.

Throughout the two millennia of Christianity, God has been
depicted in art, has been thought of and prayed to, as male. By
inference, the male image is more God-like than the female.
St Augustine, known for his misogyny, held that man alone
was the complete image of God and woman only as part of the
complementary partnership. He wrote that man was the rational
part of the image, while the woman was the bodily part!

The image of God as male has had an immense effect on both
the male and female psyche. It has even been argued that God
must be male because "He" was the biological father of Jesus by
creating a sperm in Mary's womb. And of course the resultant child,
proclaimed as the Son of God, was a male.

Jesus taught his disciples to pray to God as a Father. He himself
addressed God as Father in the familiar Aramaic term "Abba."
This was a new and challenging way of addressing God at a time
in Jewish history when God was more remote and majestic than
in previous eras. Because the Church has retained the concept of
God as "Our Father" in its worship, we might be led to believe that
this revelation about God was the ultimate stage of our spiritual
evolution. It was not. It was simply the next stage, which was
appropriate two thousand years ago.

"The faith" has frozen Jesus' words for all time and all cultures,
forgetting that he was a man of his own time and culture. This was
not meant to be the ultimate nor the total expression of Godhead.
We have to employ models to enable us to handle mysteries. It is as
if Jesus was saying: "I will give you a model of how to relate to God:
as a child does to his/her father."

Jesus did not reveal all there is to know about God. He did not,
for instance, refer to the Motherhood of God as Isaiah had done
(42:14; 66:10-14). Indeed, he said at the end of his life: "I have

much more to tell you but now it would be too much for you to bear ..." (John 16:12-13).

To get stuck at the level of a Father-child relationship to God can become a form of idolatry. We would be transforming what is no more than a model into a reality. It is not even a model that appeals to everyone. For someone who in their childhood suffered abuse from their father or stepfather, this model can be a real obstacle.

The Lord's Prayer, the "Our Father," is not the epitome of the ultimate revelation of the God-humanity relationship. In fact the prayer was only introduced into Christian liturgy in the third century, after Tertullian, a theologian from Carthage known as the "Father of Latin theology," had made the claim that it was the ultimate revelation of God.

Tomorrow's Christian appreciates that God is beyond gender. All language about God is metaphorical or analogical. It can never be a full expression. In place of those male biblical images – Lord, Judge, King, Almighty – we need to give greater worth to those biblical images of God as Life-giver, Source of vitality, Lover, Wisdom, Truth. When Jesus wept over Jerusalem at its lack of response to his Good News, he spoke of himself as a mother hen: "How often have I longed to gather your children, as a hen gathers her chicks under her wings, and you refused" (Matthew 23:37).

So long as we continue to think of and pray to God as a male, women will be less valued. This is a very important area of growth for the Church.

matters for pondering or discussion

1. Do you feel comfortable addressing God as "Father"? Have you tried thinking of God as your companion, partner in life?

2. How many biblical expressions for God can you think of which are not predominantly male? →

3. Despite the fact that the majority making up any congregation are women, the service is more than likely to be designed and conducted by a man. Is this the case in your church?

4. By whom and how are power and control exercised in your Christian community?

5. Are the services in your church predominantly based on traditional ideas?

twelve

a scriptural person ...

... recognizes that the spiritual value of the Bible lies in the present, not in the past.

Over the last century increasing numbers of Christians have moved away from the belief in the literal words of the Bible to a realization that, while it is the word of God, it is expressed in human terms, which means it has the linguistic and cultural limitations of all human communication.

There are, however, small numbers of Christians still found who regard the King James Bible as being more true to God's word than many a modern translation; who give equal weight to the Hebrew Scriptures as to the New Testament; who will take quite literally the many prohibitions and exhortations of the Old Testament as applicable today. They hold the Bible up as the ultimate authority because it is God's word. It is the content of the Bible and how it speaks to us that makes it important. It is not as if what is in it is important because it is in the Bible.

The veteran Catholic theologian of the Second Vatican Council (1962-1965) Professor Edward Schillebeeckx, wrote in his book *I am a Happy Theologian*:

> The word of God is the word of human beings who speak of God. To say, just like that, that the Bible is the word of God is simply not true ... The biblical writings are human testimonies to God ... The new theology cannot be understood without the concept of Revelation mediated by

history, of the interpretive experience of human beings.
When the mediation is not accepted, one inevitably slips
into fundamentalism.

The Anglican Archbishop Temple wrote:

> There is no such thing as revealed Truth. There are truths
> of revelation, that is to say, propositions which express the
> results of correct thinking concerning revelation; but they
> are not themselves directly revealed.

We will make the New Testament our special concern here. We
have continually to bear in mind when reading the Gospels that
the authors did not have it as their intention to write an historical
record. In no way can evangelists be compared to journalists today
who are obsessed with "facts," verifiable facts. The Gospel writers
were concerned to proclaim an experience. We all know how difficult
it is to communicate to someone else an experience that for us has
been life-changing. The evangelists were writing with the purpose
of trying to share their experience of the Jesus event with others.
While today's historians are concerned with dates and chronology,
for the evangelists this was quite unimportant, which is why we
find apparent contradictions between them. Dates and places had
to serve the proclamation of the Good News, so they were altered
accordingly – very often altered in order to give the appearance of
fulfilling a prophecy. A prophecy fulfilled provided authenticity no
matter that it had to be "bent" to fit a recorded event. There is no
way in which we can interpret the message of the Gospel writers,
coming as they did from an entirely different culture and worldview,
in the thought-forms of present-day chroniclers. In fact, to do so,
far from being faithful to God's revelation, is actually to distort the
message the written word is attempting to convey.

Then we have also to take into consideration the many stages
by which our English translations of the writings of the New
Testament have come down to us. The words I write cannot

express 100% the abstract idea I wish to communicate. What you understand from what you read is your interpretation, filtered through the background of your own experience, of what you think I am communicating. Let's apply this to the Good News of Jesus. What the Apostles understood Jesus to have said would not have been exactly what he said or meant to say. When they, in turn, preached his message they were selective, each feeding their particular audiences with what they thought their listeners should hear. Only after some decades did some of the words and actions of Jesus begin to be written down, again, selectively for different communities. Matthew, for example was writing for convert Jews so he often mentions the fulfillment of prophecies, while Mark and Luke were writing for Gentiles who had become Christians so they had to add explanations of Jewish practices. Some of the earliest texts were probably written in Aramaic (Jesus' mother tongue) which used a much more poetic form of expression than the Greek language in which the New Testament came to us. The translation from the former to the latter was a translation of thought-patterns, not simply of words. The Greek was then, centuries later, translated into Latin by St Jerome and during the Middle Ages monks copied by hand the copies of copies of this, with mistakes inevitably slipping in. From these, eventually, our different English translations were made. This is all to show that we cannot be sure exactly what words were spoken by Jesus. We have to rely on the judgment of biblical scholars – and even they are not agreed!

Having said all that we should not devalue the words of Scripture. Their value to the Christian believer today is not as an historical record but as a pointer to a way of living more fully. The Bible is one of the means by which the Spirit speaks to us today, with our culture, with our personal spiritual experience and our "scientific" knowledge. Its spiritual value does not lie in the past but in the present. Its revelatory value does not lie in a literal reading but in its application to our worldview. Just as an old map might show us the main roads but would be no help in looking for motorways or ring roads, the Bible may give us outlines but does not address current moral issues. It addressed the issues of its time. For example, polygamy was not a problem: to have lots of wives was a sign of wealth, a blessing of God. Slaves were part of the social scene. The Bible gives plenty of dietary regulations, necessary in a hot climate when there were no refrigerators.

Different Churches have different lists of the books of the Bible that they include in their Canon – that is the list of books that they accept as conveying authentic revelation. As more discoveries are made of ancient manuscripts, it is possible that in the future the Canon of the Bible will be extended to include these texts. The Gospel of Thomas is just one such.

We may have heard it said that Divine revelation ended with the death of the last Apostle, when the last word of the New Testament was written. We could be forgiven for understanding this to mean that God no longer speaks to us. True, the supreme, and in that sense ultimate, revelation of God was given to us in the person of Jesus the Christ. However, every generation – our own and future generations included – are continually coming to ever deeper understanding of the written Scriptures. The expansion of human knowledge throws new light on them. For instance, as astrophysics makes us aware of the vastness of the whole Universe, we have an understanding that the Apostles did not have: that the Jesus event was not cosmic but of concern to Planet Earth only. Our coming to know people of other religions through travel and immigration, and appreciating their religious wisdom, gives us new insights into our own religious tradition. Yes, God still speaks to us today in so many ways if we have the openness to hear Him.

The Reformed Churches claim that their faith is based solely on Scripture. Tomorrow's Christian does not accept the words of Scripture in a literal way but takes into account the background of the written word. While the left-brain person reads the Bible rationally, the right-brain person appreciates its mythical and poetic expression of truth.

matters for pondering or discussion

1. How has your own understanding of Scripture matured with the years?

2. To what extent can you say that the word of God in the Bible is your rule of life?

3. We read in Leviticus 20:13: "If a man has sexual relations with another man, they have done a disgusting thing, and both shall be put to death." If we base our condemnation of homosexual activity on the first part, why should we not take equally seriously the command to put the men to death?

4. What would you find as contradictory between what the Bible says and what today's scientists are saying? How do you handle this?

5. If you have read any of the Scriptures of other religions, what light have they shed on your own faith?

6. Is globalization leading to a single one-world faith?

thirteen

a Jesus person ...

... attempts to live by the values of Jesus of Nazareth.

"Jesus freaks," tomorrow's Christians are not! But the person of Jesus, his humanity especially, is making an increasing impact on the lives of Christians today.

Christianity is not a religion of a book, or of doctrines and dogmas and rules. These are merely props along the way. Christianity is the following of a person: Jesus.

That said, we need to acknowledge from the start that we possess very little direct, historical information about the words that are attributed to Jesus, for the reasons we saw in the previous chapter. His message was put across by his manner of living, of relating to people and by what he told them. He wrote nothing. So our accounts of him are second and third hand. Indeed, the Gospels are a mixture of history, faith, and mythical imagery. Nevertheless, because as Christians we believe that it was through this man that we receive the greatest revelation of the nature of God that we can ever receive – St Paul calls Jesus "the visible image of the invisible God" (Colossians 1:15) – it is in imitation of the values which directed his life that we come nearest to becoming the mature people God intends us to be. But notice, I do not say by imitating Jesus himself, because he lived with all the limitations of his culture, his time in history, his geographical setting. I say he invites us to live by the same values that dictated his own life. They are universal human values. His message can be summed up as:

"live your humanity fully: be the unique person you were created to be." There was nothing "out of this world" either in his own life or in the life he proposed for us all.

In this chapter I distinguish, as we always should, between the Jesus of history, who was born, grew, worked, preached, and was brutally killed, and the Christ of eternity. (I develop the theme of the Christ in a later chapter.) We are not helped to make this important distinction when so many of our public prayers – and preachers – refer to "Jesus Christ" rather than to "Jesus the Christ." "Christ" is a descriptive title, not a name, as "Jesus" is.

Jesus was a product of his times. He was a Jew and he understood that his mission was simply to reveal to his fellow Jews that there was a better, a more fulfilling way of living. "I have been sent only to the lost sheep, the people of Israel" he declared (Matthew 15:24).

For many centuries, until the last, the knowledge about Jesus that Christians were taught was "from the top downwards." By that I mean that the teaching started with God. It went something like this: God is perfect in all respects, Jesus is God, therefore Jesus is perfect in all respects. In other words, because we know what God is like, we know what Jesus was like. And so, for example, it was said that Jesus had all the Divine knowledge from the time he was born but suppressed it in his humanity. (He himself expressed his own ignorance: Matthew 24:36.) It is very hard to take as a model a person who is only "playing" at being human! The Letter to the Hebrews says: "He was tempted in every way we are, but did not sin" (4:15).

Today, theologians reverse that order. They work "from the bottom upwards." We don't know anything about God except by reflecting upon what we understand as "God in action." Watch Jesus and we get an idea of what God must be like: unconditional love.

So tomorrow's Christians are people for whom the reality of Jesus provides their guide to life. A better world cannot be built without a better people. Our primary model of what constitutes a better person is the historical figure of Jesus of Nazareth.

I suggest we can reach our best understanding of his way of life, and hence the best guidance for our own, by studying his way of relating to people. When asked, as a challenging question, what was the greatest commandment he replied: "You must love the Lord your God with all your heart, with all your soul and with all your mind. This is the greatest and the first commandment. The second resembles it: you must love your neighbor as you love yourself" (Matthew 22:37-39). Since God is unseen, the only way we can love and serve God is through our love of and service to our neighbor. The author of the First Letter of John writes: "No one has ever seen God, but if we love one another, God lives in union with us" (1 John 4:12).

Jesus grew in his appreciation of his union with God till he was able to say: "The Father and I are one" (John 10:30). He never claimed this experience was unique to himself. He regarded it as the potential of all people. His consciousness was so highly developed that he was able to see that of God in everyone. (Today we call this "Unity Consciousness," as experienced by mystics.) This is what characterized all his relationships.

In Jesus' time, as in our own, people's worth was estimated by their effectiveness in society. There was in consequence a hierarchy of importance. Children were non-persons, women not much less. The deformed, the possessed, public sinners, the lepers were all outcasts, of no value to society so of no worth. Jesus was able to recognize the presence of the Divine in every person he encountered. No one was of no value, because their value lay within themselves, in their divinity. His acting upon this insight caused him to turn all the social values of his culture upside-down. He ate with sinners, he mixed with Gentiles, he touched the unclean, he invited children to come to him. He restored to everyone a sense of their own worth and dignity. He gave hope to the hopeless. He described his vision for the world with the metaphor of the "Kingdom of God," describing how such a world would be if only God were allowed to be in charge.

He spoke of the sort of world that could be if everyone related to everyone else in the same way he did, with unconditional love, recognizing the Divine presence in even the seemingly most unlikely. First of all, through recognizing the Divine presence within ourselves.

What a model for us who profess to be Jesus people! What a different world this could be. How can we persecute, torture, kill another human being, or fail to nourish the most abandoned, when we perceive them as being vessels of the Divine as we ourselves are.

In short, tomorrow's Christians are deriving more inspiration for life as they come to know Jesus of Nazareth, than they did from the Jesus they were offered in the past who, as the Christ, is the Second person of the Blessed Trinity.

matters for pondering or discussion

1. Have you ever read, or heard a recording of a single Gospel right through continuously? It throws up many insights that we miss when only hearing a small portion read in church.

2. Which is your favorite Gospel? Why do you resonate with this one?

3. Do you give more importance to the Christmas story or the passion and death story than to the intervening years of Jesus' ministry?

4. If you pray to Jesus, what image of him do you have?

5. If you possess pictures or a statue of Jesus, are they a help to understanding the historical person?

6. Did you ever think of "Jesus" as a first name and "Christ" as a surname? Do you still do so?

fourteen

a challenging person ...

... challenges institutional evil.

To pronounce oneself a Christian is to claim to be a follower of Jesus the Christ. We in our western society, living two thousand years later, are not called to live as Jesus of Nazareth lived in his time, his culture, with his limited technological knowledge. But we are called to live by the values which dictated his way of living and relating and which he preached as that Good News which would set us free from our inner slaveries to "become mature people, reaching the very height of the Christ's full stature" (Ephesians 4:13).

I am often asked why it was that since Jesus was to make known to humanity that God had a plan for us and what that plan was – so beautifully expressed in Ephesians 1:10: ("This plan which God will complete when the time is right, is to bring all creation together, everything in the heavens and on Earth, with the Christ as head.") – that it is only in the last minutes, so to speak, of human history, that Jesus of Nazareth appeared on the scene. The answer I give is that, previous to that moment, human consciousness had not developed sufficiently either to give Jesus himself the insights he had or for humanity to take on board the radical message he proclaimed.

And radical it was! Jesus was no "Yes man." He was not "a pillar of society." In the eyes of the religious leaders of the time he was a heretic, and a dangerous heretic at that. He broke both the religious laws and the social customs. His message was so contrary to what was generally acceptable that we have to admit that today – two thousand years later – there are or have been very few Christians who have taken his message to heart in such a way that they have stood out from society as a challenge to our settled way of life.

Christians will always be a minority in the world, today forming only a sixth of the world's population. Tomorrow's Christians no longer regard the reason for their being a Christian as that of saving their souls. Being a Christian means being a witness to others that there are higher values which should dictate our lives.

If we are to be people who challenge society with these higher values, it means that in the first place we ourselves must be prepared to be challenged. Jesus did not come to give comforting words, at least not as we usually understand the word "comfort." From its Latin roots it means "com-fort": "with strength." Jesus said he came to bring the sword, that his followers would cause divisions within their own families. Not much comfort in that! Jesus was a challenger.

As his followers, his voice in our world, tomorrow's Christians are called to challenge institutional injustice, as Jesus did, as much in the realm of religion as in society at large. For instance, the right wing of the Church – the wealthiest constituency – is obsessed with sexuality issues, while ignoring what Jesus said about the danger of riches. As someone has said: if Jesus were alive today he would be more concerned with what went on in the boardroom than in the bedroom! Jesus hardly spoke about human sexuality but he had a great deal to say about the injustices of the system. He was in line with the great prophets of Israel who challenged their people with substituting religious ritual and purity for the concerns of God, which were more about justice to the poor than the collection of religious offerings.

To challenge society on social justice issues is to invite unpopularity. We put ourselves on the margins. Our greatest fear is to be disapproved of. We work hard at becoming acceptable. But this is the fate of the true prophetic figure. This is what it means for tomorrow's Christian: to be challenged by the message of Jesus and in turn to challenge the injustices in our present world. We can only take the risk of challenging society if we feel secure in ourselves, centered and well-grounded. And one of the most powerful means of gaining this inner strength is through the daily practice of contemplative meditation.

Today the question we might be faced with is whether to support an appeal for a new church organ or promote an appeal for funds to dig more wells in African villages. Or how to go about influencing fair trade in the world for the benefit of developing countries.

When we are faced with a challenging moral decision where no clear-cut answer is obvious, a quick rule of thumb is to ask: will this action be life-enhancing or life-draining? Will this action make me and others more loving or less loving?

If we are simply free-wheeling Christians we can so easily fall into the trap of colluding with the system, of which we are a part, and which oppresses others. We collude by doing and saying nothing. For there to be any change, these systems have to be challenged. This is what it means to exercise our prophetic ministry.

matters for pondering or discussion

1. Can you recall an occasion when you have not spoken out against the majority view for what you considered to be an injustice? How did you feel about that?

2. Name some of the injustices you feel are practised within the Church today.

3. Are you yourself open to having your views challenged by others?

4. Read the Sermon on the Mount (Matthew chapters 5 to 7) and write down on which points you feel Jesus' words are challenging your present life. →

5. Would you say that your church forms part of global capitalism?

fifteen

a prophetic person ...

... is constantly evaluating the trends in society.

Few of us would think of ourselves as prophets. This is because the title is usually associated with foretelling the future, often a future of doom or disaster.

Yet being a Christian entails being a prophet in another sense. And at no time is this more needed than in our present chaotic world. In the Christian context the role of prophet is to ponder the events of our time and to discern whether or not what we might call "the hand of God" is in them. And then to pronounce upon the fact. This idea needs some unpacking.

We are not, in the first place, Christians who inhabit the world but rather we are citizens of the world who are Christians. We represent some one-sixth of the present six billion people living on this planet. We are not people divorced from this world but have our feet as firmly on the ground as everyone else. What distinguishes us is that we have chosen to live with a particular philosophy, a particular interpretation of what life is all about, which is inspired by our belief that there is an ultimate love which we name God, that there is a purpose for creation and a destiny for every human being beyond this present life. We believe, further, that God is under-girding these purposes, not by direct intervention, but through human instrumentality. If, as Christians, we accept being partners with God in this evolutionary process, we have to be continually alert to what is going on in our world and equally alert to detect any signs that through these events the God-willed purpose is coming about. In other words, we have continually to be "reading the signs of the times."

The expression "signs of the times" is frequently used in everyday parlance to refer to current trends, for instance, the rise in the cost of living or the mounting violence or the increasing lack of respect for authority. But the phrase has a specific biblical meaning. That is, signs of God's continuous active presence in the world manifest through human agencies. It is in this sense that Jesus used the expression when he was challenged by the religious leaders.

> Some Pharisees and Sadducees who came to Jesus wanted
> to trap him, so they asked him to perform a miracle
> for them, to show that God approved of him. But Jesus
> answered: "When the sun is setting you say 'We are going
> to have fine weather because the sky is red.' And early in the
> morning you say 'It is going to rain because the sky is red
> and dark.' You can predict the weather by looking at the sky,
> but you cannot interpret the signs of the times" (Matthew
> 16:1-3).

The sign the Pharisees and Sadducees were unwilling to recognize was how God was active through Jesus' very mission.

To live Christianly is to live perpetually examining the trends in society and making a judgment about them based upon God's revelation in Scripture of the sort of world that God delights in. The world's Catholic Bishops expressed this succinctly when they met for the Second Vatican Council (1962-1965):

> The People of God ... motivated by faith, labors to decipher
> authentic signs of God's presence and purpose in the
> happenings, needs and desires in which this People has a
> part along with other people of our age'. (*Gaudium et Spes*.
> N.11)

It is not an exercise that we might indulge in from time to time. It is a way of life. The German theologian Karl Barth wrote that the Christian should pray with a Bible in one hand and the newspaper in the other. It should become a habit that each time we listen to the news on the radio we ask ourselves: What are the values behind this event, this speech, this decision?

But that is the first stage only. From the variety of items of news we hear, can we discern trends in society? Trends are ways of thinking or acting which are becoming increasingly or decreasingly widespread. What are the undercurrents we notice today that will become the tidal wave of tomorrow? Do we spot trends that we can recognize as furthering God's design for the world or are they such that they militate against it?

The role of the prophet – the role of every Christian who is concerned to bring about a better world – is to announce and support those trends which are furthering the Kingdom of God and similarly to denounce and oppose those which are destructive of this design.

The task of prophecy is distributed throughout the Christian community. As well as discerning the trends, each of us has to discern our unique calling. Which are the trends, relating to my talents and abilities, that I am being called to champion, and which not? We each have to trust to others the work that is theirs.

We cannot all be banner-carrying militants, but each of us, in our own corner, can make our views known whenever a contemporary subject is raised. Advocacy by letter-writing, whether to our Member of Parliament or to a broadcasting station or to the Chief Executive of a corporation, as well as giving support to the hundreds of organizations that exist to further this or that concern, are all ways in which tomorrow's Christians can exercise their prophetic calling, and so make a difference, make our world ever so slightly better.

matters for pondering or discussion

1. See if you can compose a list of contemporary trends in each of the following aspects of life: Political, Social, Economic, Scientific, Religious.

2. Mark against each trend whether it favors Kingdom values or is contrary to Kingdom values. (Note some may be neutral in themselves, the value coming from the use made of them.)

3. Christians have been called "artisans of a new humanity." What action can you take to support any of the positive trends or to oppose the negative?

4. To what extent do you find yourself being caught up unwittingly in a current trend, which, upon consideration, you would oppose?

5. Are prophets favored in your church?

sixteen

a community person ...

... experiences growth within a small group of like-minded people.

The emerging of certain forms of Protestantism following the Reformation emphasized the individual conscience of Christians. Methodism and Pietism re-emphasized personal guilt, personal experience, and individual perfection. This emphasis on individual salvation was also shared by the Anglican and Catholic Churches until the middle of the last century. Then the pendulum began to swing the other way, toward the communitarian dimension of Christianity and it is this emphasis on the community aspect that is a characteristic of the life of tomorrow's Christians.

In this regard, we need to make the distinction between spirituality and religion. Today it is generally recognized in the West that people are becoming less and less religious. Church attendance is falling, the Christian heritage of our culture is being forgotten or ignored, the influence the Church once had over our moral values and public conduct has almost disappeared. On the other hand, more people are discovering that this loss causes a vacuum in their lives. They are searching for that spiritual dimension which gives meaning to life, and the search takes them in a thousand different directions, many of which are labeled "New Age." Despite the diversity of its manifestations, I suggest "spirituality" may be thought of as that aspect of our nature – related to the physical and psychological aspects – which awakens us to wonder, gives our lives meaning, and calls us toward our higher self, usually expressed as a relationship with the Transcendent, sometimes named "God." This is spirituality defined in the most universal terms. For the Christian it is more directed. It is the pursuit of those values which are manifested in the life and teaching of Jesus the Christ, which give meaning and direction to one's life, calling one toward union with God and, through God, with all creation.

Spirituality is part of our very make-up as human beings, whether recognized or not. It is our individual journey of discovery and pursuit of life's purpose. People live their spirituality whether or not they adhere to any particular religion.

"Religion," by contrast, is of its very nature communitarian because it consists of a particular framework (which usually includes four elements: a belief system, a moral code, an authority structure, and a form of worship) within which people find nourishment for the spiritual dimension of their lives and explore their spiritual journey in the company of others. They do so by free choice. They embrace that "religious" way of life, which has been developed over centuries by their spiritual ancestors. Those who choose the Christian religion have elected to take on board the beliefs, practices, morality, and values lived as Church in a particular cultural context.

Many Christians resource their spiritual lives through their participation in a parish or church congregation. It becomes the focus of their Church membership. Such a grouping of Christians has a sociological origin, not a biblical one. There is no mention of the parish in the New Testament. After all, Jesus did not have the intention of founding a Church, just as he had no intention of launching a new religion upon the world. As we have already seen, the Good News centered on what Jesus called the Kingdom of God.

The cultural context in the West today is moving toward community. This is not a new movement. Human beings have from the earliest days realized the necessity for survival of living together in groups. Ever since, there has been a process by which these groups have chosen to be attached to bigger and bigger groups.

Nomadic groups settled into village life and formed clans and clans identified themselves as belonging to a tribe. Tribes united to form nations. Nations went out to establish empires. Today we speak of the planet as our Global Village and of "globalization," whether of commerce, or multiculturalism, or multi-ethnicity.

What is new is a parallel reverse movement. Curiously, it is precisely the growth of larger and larger "communities" that is causing people to feel a loss of identity. So, simultaneously there is a movement toward re-forming previous small nations, not as a movement for independence, but to give their citizens a feeling of belonging.

In the West we have lost all the safeguards and buffers that our ancestors had in their extended family. Today's members of nuclear families search for a replacement of this, and they are finding it in membership of small communities of such a size that everyone knows everyone else and where all rally round to support a suffering member. These may be life-enhancing groups or task-orientated groups. They may be found geographically among those who flee city living to village life, or in common interest groups such as clubs and societies, or among those engaged collaboratively for a campaign.

Today the movement is happening within the Churches too. In the western world in the Middle Ages, each village community had a church as the center of its common life. Villages were small, everyone was a Christian, everyone knew everyone else. It was a mutually supportive community. With the rise of urbanization, starting three centuries ago, the church building served a much larger group, such that in many cases there is no way individuals can now know more than a small number in their congregation. And further, Christian life, as expressed through the local church, had less and less relevance to the secular aspects of life, of which many concerns have today been embraced by social services.

As an organizational structure that has remained largely unchanged over four hundred years, one has to ask whether, in today's social pattern, the parish is fulfilling the purpose for which it was originally established. Witness the number of small parish churches with diminishing congregations where the energy of the group is not being invigorated by the structure of the parish but, on the contrary, is being diminished, sucked away, by the necessity to raise money to maintain a culturally beautiful but contemporarily redundant church building.

Apart from the historical fact of four hundred years of unchanged structure, the concept of parish needs to be rethought. There are existential, cultural, and sociological reasons why tomorrow's Christians are seeking a change. The existential fact is that church congregations are dwindling. The parish is not answering the relationship needs of people and is seen by the majority who call themselves Christians as isolated from everyday life. The cultural reason for change is on account of the widening gap between the Church as an institution – that is, how it understands itself – and what non-members see and experience. To many it appears to belong to a past culture. Finally, the sociological reason for restructuring the parish is that today, in the West, where the extended family living in proximity has disappeared, people are looking for human-sized communities, of, for example, some twenty people, to whom they can relate at depth about all the concerns of their life, spiritual and secular. Such small communities, falling as they do between the small nuclear family and the large anonymous congregation, enable their members to be known, to be appreciated, to feel needed. In fact they provide the secure company of others in which to nurture the fullness of their Christian life.

So large anonymous congregations are restructuring themselves into neighborhood groups. The Churches which provide the warmest welcome into their community are the ones that are attracting new members, especially the young.

The formation of these small Christian communities, networking with others to form a communion of communities, will enable the Church to move from a hierarchical structure of authority to a community model. The existing parish becomes the focal point of such a network and provides the services which are beyond the ability or competence of the neighborhood community to provide.

So, many who at present are passive in their church attendance feel freer to participate in a small community where they know they are appreciated for who they are rather than for what they can do. It is in experiencing the safety of such a community that we find ourselves in the most propitious environment for personal growth. Among sympathetic friends we can let fall the pretences and be our real selves. A South African proverb says: "A person is a person because of other people." The deepest desire of our real self is to grow, to overcome fears, to become more.

And yet the small community is not simply a mini parish. It is a group of people who are concerned that every member is encouraged to minister to others in whatever way they are able or willing, and to accept the ministry of others. By contrast, the parish is usually led by one or several ordained ministers and is concerned more with programs and activities. While the parish aims to recruit people into the congregation, the small community is concerned to go out to befriend and serve people in their neighborhood. Not so as to attract them into the church but because it is the Christian thing to do. In a nutshell: while the parish is Church-orientated, the small Christian community is Kingdom-orientated.

The fact that on every continent today, for differing reasons, churches are restructuring themselves into communions of basic communities is surely a sign that the Holy Spirit is nudging the Church into a new shape, the more competently to answer today's needs.

matters for pondering or discussion

1. List the groups or clubs you belong to – secular or religious. What benefits are you deriving from your membership of each? What contribution are you able to make to each?

→

2. Is your religious life something you prefer to keep to yourself?

3. If you are a churchgoer, do you feel at home, free to be yourself, in your present parish congregation? Does it encourage honesty and vulnerability?

4. Is your congregation outer-directed or inward-looking? Is there evidence of control by a few?

5. If you think the establishment of small neighborhood communities within your parish will bring forth more participation, how will you go about presenting the idea to your clergy and parish council?

seventeen

a church person ...

... feels a responsibility to re-vision the Church.

The very word "church" conjures up so many ideas, different emotions. To many, it simply means a building. Here we reflect not on Churches as denominations but on the local Christian community. We may define it as the community of followers of Jesus the Christ with a mission to be a sign to the world, by the example of its way of life, of the unity to which all humanity is called: a unity with God, with each other, and with the whole of creation. In current parlance this community is labeled "Church." A good starting point for our reflection is the statement by Bishop John Spong: "The business of the Church is to love people into life." All else is a means to that end.

Jesus did not found a Church, certainly not the Church as we experience it today. He left us no directions about the organization or structure of the community of his followers. The Church as we know it owes more to the mission of St Paul than to the apostles who remained in Jerusalem. Paul proclaimed the "Good News" about Jesus to the different peoples, with their various cultures, in the territories of the Eastern Mediterranean. Each community responded to his announcement in its own cultural way and formed itself into the community shape which they felt was the most appropriate to live out their response, the most appropriate structure for living and witnessing this new way of life that Jesus had introduced. Today's missionaries have a word for this process:

they call it "inculturation." That is, announcing the Good News of the gospel in terms meaningful to each culture and encouraging each culture to respond to it in their own way. But inculturation does not work simply horizontally – between today's different cultures on different continents – but also vertically through history. In other words, it is equally necessary for tomorrow's Christians in our western society to be able to respond to the proclamation of the gospel in a way that relates authentically with their everyday lives. If the structure of the Christian community, the language it uses, and the manner of its worship do not feed people's spiritual needs today, then it is presenting itself as an outdated culture, of benefit to only a small minority of traditionalists.

As with all institutions, the local Church's structures have frequently to be reviewed. They were formed in a past age to answer a past need of a past people. If they remain in that form as if hallowed by history, all the energy of the dwindling community is channeled into preserving the structure, whereas the structure of any community has only one purpose: to be life-giving or task-enabling.

Let us take one example. The majority of Christian Churches today maintain a hierarchical structure. In other words, they have a pyramid shape with authority established at the peak, and this trickles down, layer by layer of office-holders, until it reaches the general membership, the laity, at the base. Why is this so?

The Christian message was launched on the western world by St Paul into a society that was subject to the Roman Empire. As the numbers grew they required a regulating structure to give them cohesion. The community took on the pyramidal structure of the Empire. It knew no other. The same structure is with us still in most Churches, in greater or lesser degree, as it is still the structure of secular society.

Yet if we read the Gospels with this thought in mind, we find that Jesus had a very different vision for his followers. Status, learning, title meant nothing to him. "The greatest among you must be your servant" he said (Matthew 23:11) and he gave them an illustration of what this meant by getting down on his knees and washing his disciples' feet during the Last Supper.

This challenges the structures of leadership within our respective Churches. The role of the minister, the priest in the community of tomorrow's Christians is that of facilitator, enabling each member to exercise their talents for the good of all. No one leader is an expert in every avenue of leadership. The facilitator is the point of unity of the community who enables different members to exercise leadership of the group in their particular area of expertise or experience.

If the Christian community's mission is to be a sign to the world, it is to be a sign that there is a different set of values by which we are invited to live. These are the values that Jesus described with the metaphor of the Kingdom of God: a world that is driven by internal spiritual values, not by those of greed, individualism, and struggle for economic or political power.

Tomorrow's Christians are called to re-vision the Church. Only when the Jesus vision is re-expressed in today's cultural terms will it appeal to a people suffering from anxiety, desperation, insecurity, and confusion. To quote Bishop John Spong again: "The task of the Church becomes less that of indoctrinating or relating people to an external divine power and more that of providing opportunities for people to touch the infinite center of all things and to grow into all that they are destined to be."

matters for pondering or discussion

1. What Church structures do you think need to be re-evaluated so that they are life-supporting and not life-draining?

2. What move can you make to encourage such an evaluation?

3. What are the areas in which you can say your Church community is giving a collective witness of a gospel way of life? Have you heard anybody remark upon it?

→

4. Is the language used by your Christian community, in explaining its beliefs and in its prayers and preaching, understandable to the average tabloid newspaper reader?

5. Does your community give out signals of hope in your neighborhood? Does it address your neighbors' daily problems?

eighteen

a mission person ...

... wishes to share with others the vision of what the world could be like.

U nlike the other great religions – until recent years at least – a unique characteristic of Christianity is that from the earliest days it saw itself as having a missionary purpose. That is to say, it considered itself to be the unique way to salvation and the path to salvation lay in being converted to Christianity and consequently becoming a Church member.

That mission is an indisputable task for the Church has been based upon what is called the "Great Commission": Jesus' final instruction to his disciples: "Go then to all peoples everywhere and make them my disciples" – at least that is according to Matthew (28:19). However, as we know, there are very few words reported of Jesus that we can be certain he spoke. These are not among them. What is evident from other sayings of Jesus (both from Matthew) is that he saw himself as having a mission only to his fellow Jews:

> These twelve men were sent out by Jesus with the following instructions: "Do not go to any Gentile territory or any Samaritan towns. Instead, you are to go to those lost sheep, the people of Israel." (10:5-6)

and:

> "I have been sent only to those lost sheep, the people of Israel." (15:24)

Matthew's Gospel was written after the fall of Jerusalem, after CE 70, which is twenty years after what has been named the "Council of Jerusalem" (about CE 49). This Council attempted to heal the rift caused by two opposing views about the future of the Christian community. On the one side was the Jerusalem community led by James, "the brother of Jesus," the Aramaic-speaking Christians – known as "The Hebrews" (Acts 6:1) – who believed that Jesus had no other intention than to renew his own religion, and on the other, the Greek-speaking Jewish Christians – the Hellenists – led by Paul and his disciples who, supported by a vision that Peter had seen (Acts 10), understood that the Jesus message was for all races. Had Jesus' command, as reported by Matthew (28:19), been original the dispute that nearly split the young Church would not have occurred.

But with the Great Commission taken literally throughout a large part of the Church's history, one can understand that for most of this period the Church traded on the phrase of first-century Ignatius of Antioch: "Outside the Church no salvation." Right up to the nineteenth century the missionary thrust which spawned the birth of so many missionary societies, founded to follow the great explorers into new territories, was all about baptizing the "natives" and so saving their souls. This task was named the "Foreign Missions." The implication was that we "civilized" people in the West had "the Truth" and were going to give it to the "ignorant pagans." This approach lasted till the middle of the last century.

It was slowly recognized that the so-called pagans also had a long religious heritage: they were not without a sense of God (by whatever name) in their lives. It was not a case of "we have the Truth; you are in error." Missionaries began to appreciate that the message they took was not one-directional. The people they were among gave them new insights into their own faith. Their calling began to be named "overseas mission." Today, with our multi-ethnic, multi-religious societies in all countries, the task has come to be known as "cross-cultural mission."

While the Church still rightly claims: "The Church exists for mission," the meaning of mission has changed. No longer is the movement inward, that of attracting people into the Church, but outward, as a community that witnesses to society what life could be like if we all lived by the values of Jesus of Nazareth, the values of the Kingdom of God.

A distinction has been developing over these last decades between what is called "Evangelization" and "Evangelism." The former is the interaction of the gospel on culture; the latter is a call to personal commitment to following the Christ. Evangelization is accomplished by the actions and lifestyle of the community as well as by proclamation, rather than the person-to-person encounter, usually by word of mouth, of evangelism. While this latter presents a personal challenge because the intended outcome is conversion, the former is carried out in dialogue – listening, accompanying, sharing – so the outcome is unpredictable. Evangelization, concerned with communitarian salvation, holiness, and spirituality, changes the emphasis from "saving souls" to integral salvation; it is Kingdom of God centered. Evangelism, while it reaches out to present Church members, to non-churchgoing Christians and to non-Christians, is Church centered and concerned with the salvation of individuals. One can say Evangelism is predominantly the approach of the Evangelical Alliance Churches, while Evangelization is that of the Catholic Church and World Council of Churches. These two approaches are not opposed to each other; they should complement each other.

Tomorrow's Christian has a vision of what the world could be like, and this she longs to share. But her sharing is in dialogue (as we will describe in the next chapter), with openness to receive as well as to give, with respect, and with no sense that we are right while others, because they think differently, are in error.

Our way of mission is by witness and our witness is in the way we project ourselves as a Christian community. "See how they love one another." At the end of his life Jesus prayed, according to John: "I pray that they all may be one, Father … May they be one so that the world will believe that you sent me" (17:21). Who is not attracted by a loving, caring, compassionate, welcoming group? That is mission for this century. Not mission to increase Church membership but mission for the Kingdom of God on Earth. We witness the Good News of Jesus, not in order to make Christians, but to change the world.

matters for pondering or discussion

1. What has been your reaction when you have been approached by an evangelist asking: "Are you saved?" And what was your reply?

2. Do you think the Church should continue to "convert" people of other religions?

3. It is said: "Spirituality unites: Religion divides." If you think this is true, what form should the Church's mission take today?

4. Which would you rate the more urgent task to address our world's needs – Evangelization or Evangelism?

nineteen

a peace-making person ...

... speaks the truth in a spirit of love.

No one can call our world a peaceful place. There can be no peace without justice. There can be no justice without a willingness to share. There can be no sharing without an experience of community. There can be no community without peace. So we find ourselves in a vicious circle. Yet all these elements are at the very heart of Kingdom-living, of the life of tomorrow's Christian.

The prerequisite for our effectiveness as peacemakers is to work on our own inner peace, our peace of mind, our peace of heart. A person living in deep peace exudes peace.

We must distinguish between a peacemaker and a peace-keeper. The latter looks for "peace at any price." Keep your head down. Don't disturb the status quo. Don't challenge the situation. Anything for a quiet life.

The peacemaker envisages how things could be different. She takes the initiative, takes a risk, challenges a person or a situation. It is not an easy option, but it is the Christian means of bringing about a better world. It was the Jesus method.

If we have a Christian love for other people then we will see them through the same eyes as Jesus did. He saw the Divine presence in everyone. He saw the enormous potential for good in each person, the ember that only needed fanning to bring it into flame. And he was not afraid to challenge whatever he saw to be enchaining people and preventing them from living a fully human life.

The fundamental attitude of the peacemaker is the appreciation of what we all have in common rather than concern for the little that differentiates us. At the physical level, as human beings, apart from a few external features (color of skin, type of hair, shape of head, stature, etc) our bodies are 99.9% the same, no matter what part of the world we come from, as indeed they have been over thousands and thousands of years. Spiritually too, the deepest aspirations of every person – for love, for peace, for fulfillment, for becoming more – are the same. Despite all the negative behavior of people, which we see in the media, there is so much goodness in every human being that it would take a lifetime to appreciate.

The most effective tool at our disposal for being a peacemaker is dialogue. Dialogue has been succinctly defined by the writer of the Letter to the Ephesians as "Speaking the truth in a spirit of love" (4:15). This shows up the difference between debate and dialogue. In debate we are trying to win a point, to convert the other to our way of thinking or acting. It is confrontational: "I am right, you are wrong." In dialogue we are disposed to hear and weigh up the other's point of view, we are open to new creative possibilities, open to being changed as a consequence. The former injures relationships; the latter deepens them. In debate we are like boxers. In dialogue we are like dancers.

A degree of acceptance and trust has to be present for us to feel we can speak out our truth. This cannot be expected on every occasion. There are some people to whom we feel close – as children toward parents – but without necessarily feeling free with them. With others, with whom, for instance, we are on the same wavelength, we can feel free to share at a deep level even without being close to them. With casual acquaintances we feel neither free nor close, whereas with a very small number of people we are able to feel both close and free. We have to allow for, and not be surprised by, the psychology of relationships when attempting to "speak the truth in a spirit of love." There is a time and a place to speak.

If our attempt to dialogue with people of a different persuasion has as its intention to give those people our mutual support and encouragement to live a more fulfilled life, then we can say that at least we have made the attempt to be peacemakers.

What we say here about dialogue between individuals applies equally to dialogue between the world's religions. Religion is one of the most prominent causes of prejudices, factions, and wars in our present world. That which professes to "bring peace to all men" is so often the very cause of conflict.

matters for pondering or discussion

1. Can you say you help to create a climate in which dialogue can happen?

2. Do you listen to people with your heart as well as with your ears?

3. Can you name people whom you feel dominate or inhibit you? Do you love them enough to be able to tell them how you feel toward them?

4. List the fears that prevent you taking the risk to be a peacemaker in a given situation?

5. Would you feel secure enough in yourself to raise or discuss these questions in a group?

6. Is your church a peacemaking church?

twenty

a spiritual experience person ...

... needs no external authority to validate personal belief.

Within the different strands of Christianity there are two opposite opinions held as to what should be the basis of our belief. There are those who teach that sound belief can only be based on objective truth, which is found in Divine revelation as expressed in the Bible and in the traditional interpretation of the Bible. The other school teaches that one's ultimate authority for accepting Christian teaching is a personal spiritual experience.

There are loyal churchgoing Christians who observe faithfully the law of God as taught by the Church and carry out all their religious practices punctiliously, but whose religious life is lived at a surface level because their heart is not touched: they have not had an experience of God. They know a great deal *about* God, but they do not "know" God. On the other hand, one meets people who have had a deep spiritual experience. The Alister Hardy Religious Experience Research Centre claims in its publicity flyer:

> More than half the adult population of Britain believe
> that they have had spiritual or transcendent experiences,
> such as an awareness of a supernatural presence or power,
> meaningful patterning of events, extra-sensory perception,
> a feeling of guidance or answer to prayer. Often these
> experiences are of immense personal significance and alter
> the course of people's lives.

Yet they may have had no religious roots within which to ground that experience and therefore they have no way of giving it meaning, of interpreting it, or of fitting it into a mental framework by which it can be a means of spiritual growth.

Those who teach the necessity of objective revelation as the basis of belief need to recall that the Bible itself is nothing other than a record of human experience, as we saw in a previous chapter.

All the major religions came into being because their founder had a profound, what we might call "revelationary," spiritual experience. Jesus himself had such a vivid consciousness of God that he explained it as God-in-him: "The Father and I are one" (John 10:30). Furthermore, acknowledging the fact that it is the same God who empowers everyone, we must accept the validity of the spiritual experience of the followers of other religions. Although the intensity or circumstances of the experience may differ, and indeed how it is described, in essence it is the same for all: an experience of the Divine. Where we part company is in the interpretation of that experience, which will depend on the religious framework we accept as giving our lives meaning. One person may name the vision of a Divine being as Jesus, another as Krishna.

In the past a great weight was placed on Christian apologetics: the provision of rational arguments to prove the existence of God. Anyone who has had a direct experience of God is in no need of such rationalizing. In any case, it is simply not possible to prove the existence of God in such a form that is acceptable to all. Reasonable, well-informed, and sensitive thinkers are able to produce rational arguments to prove that God does, or equally to prove that God does not, exist. One of the greatest theological minds in the history of the Church, Thomas Aquinas, who applied Aristotelian logic to rationalize Christian beliefs had a mystical experience toward the end of his life, in comparison with which, he wrote: "All I have written seems like so much straw."

The great mystics in the Church's history have not been popular with the ecclesiastical hierarchy because their spiritual experience was such that their faith was self-affirming. It did not require authenticating by any external authority.

In our own times many people are putting more emphasis on subjective experience than on objective doctrine as a guide to life. We notice the rise in reports of people having out-of-the-body or near-death experiences, which have caused them to have a completely different attitude to life, a realization that the human being is more than just body and mind: that our consciousness is not to be equated with the brain but can operate outside and beyond the body. This experience is giving a reality to the Christian's belief in life after death.

For tomorrow's Christians the ultimate authority for accepting the validity of Christian belief is not the word of ecclesiastical authority – needful though that is for guidance – but personal spiritual experience. Bishop Richard Holloway writes: "Experiences of God are self-evidencing to the participant. They operate within their own integrity, follow the logic of their own experience and require no external authority to validate them; they validate themselves."

From what is said above, it might be inferred that a spiritual experience is always extraordinary, a peak experience. But this is only one aspect. The Spirit can be experienced in any situation. She can be experienced in ordinary everyday life, in love, in compassion, in pain and hardship, even in the chasm of despair. The Spirit never abandons us. She can break through into our lives at the oddest moments. Sadly, we are not always open receivers.

matters for pondering or discussion

1. Why are you a Christian?

2. Make a chart of the high points and low points in the spiritual journey of your life.

→

3. Can you claim that you have had a spiritual experience that has been "of immense personal significance" and altered the course of your life?

4. Do you find it hard to accept that the spiritual experience of someone of another religion is as valid as your own?

5. Would you say you "know" God?

twenty-one

a mystery person ...

... puts the pursuit of wisdom above the pursuit of knowledge.

Tomorrow's Christians live with mystery. This is not to say they are a mysterious people! The western mind is uncomfortable with mystery. Ever since the period in our history named the Enlightenment – the eighteenth-century philosophical movement stressing the supremacy of reason – we look for certainty. Scientists carry out the same experiments time and time again to reach certainty about their theories.

Today, with the uncertainty caused by the increasing rapidity of change, there are those who look for certainty in religious matters, hoping for some unchanging spiritual rock on which to anchor themselves. The many Christians among them look for this in the Bible, taking its contents literally "because it is the word of God." They are named Fundamentalists or Literalists. They convince themselves that certainty about how to conduct their lives lies in the literal application of the commands of Scripture. "It must be right because it is directly inspired by God." (But we cannot help noticing that a lot of picking and choosing goes on! For example, Exodus 21:7 allows a man to sell his daughter as a slave. Many of us work on Sundays but Exodus 35:2 clearly states that anyone who works on the Sabbath should be put to death. How many Literalists enjoy their dish of scampi, yet Leviticus 11:10 says eating shellfish is an abomination.)

We in the West feel uneasy with uncertainty. So we search for

Truth. But Truth is not an end in itself; it is a means to an end. It enables us to become more loving people. We grow into union with God by becoming more loving people, not by becoming more knowledgeable.

Truth is a mystery. As one author has said, one of the great mysteries of faith is the mystery of faith! Faith is what enables us to live with uncertainty. If we had certainty we would have no need of faith. We live our lives on the edge of the unknown – in mystery. Mystery cannot be captured or preserved or controlled. It can only be known in the heart of a person. It is not the Agatha Christie type of mystery. We do not come to Truth by searching for more clues. It is no use waiting for the next generation of scientists to discover the mystery of Truth. It is a mystery in the sense that it is beyond our minds to comprehend in totality.

We deceive ourselves that we know all about God when we describe God as a Trinity of persons. What we know about the Trinity is very little and very baffling – once we have departed from the mathematical. But with it we are trying in a limited human fashion to express something that is at the very center of the Godhead, not because we need to know this about God, but because we need to know it to tell us something about ourselves. It tells us why we are attracted to community. It assures us of the power behind our puny efforts to make the Kingdom a reality.

Many Christians call for hierarchical pronouncements or for catechisms because they expect everything to be spelt out in black and white. But there are more gray areas than black and white, especially in the field of morality, in which new dilemmas are frequently appearing, for which there is no straightforward, certainly no biblical, answer. Those Churches that publish a catechism risk doing their membership a disservice. They are attempting to remove the reality of mystery. They act as parents toward children who beg for answers. They are emphasizing the importance of knowledge and thereby diminishing the growth of wisdom.

The human mind is simply not capable of grasping Truth in its entirety. Only the God-mind has the fullness of Truth. In our human state we can only handle Truth partially, as truths: the different aspects of Truth. Imagine Truth like a multi-faced crystal globe, each side representing a truth. However much we keep turning it around we can never do more than perceive a few sides at a time. Never the whole at once.

To deny the mystery element in religion is to deprive ourselves of the ability to wonder. Wonder is a child-like quality, which in our adult life, with our desire for knowing facts and figures, we so easily lose. Knowledge, we tell ourselves, is power. It contains an element of control. We have to free ourselves from the need to know, from that particular slavery. We enter mystery through our intuition, not through our reasoning. Knowledge tends to deaden, mystery to enlighten. Mystery moves us from knowledge to wisdom. What is required is that we contemplate mystery. We can convey wisdom through symbols, analogies, art. It cannot be pinned down. Without mystery we are impoverished. Einstein said: "The most beautiful thing we can experience is the mysterious."

Tomorrow's Christians recognize that no religion has the fullness of Truth. Just as no culture has a monopoly of wisdom. All are but partial experiences of the Divine Mystery. Eckhart Tolle has written: "Wisdom is not a product of thought. The deep *knowing* that is wisdom arises through the simple act of giving someone or something your full attention."

We can only enter into the Divine Mystery by contemplation.

matters for pondering or discussion

1. Do you feel an insecurity in not having rational certainty about some religious truths? Which?

2. Have you tried to "understand" the Mystery of the Trinity? The Trinity is a human way of expressing the inexpressible mystery of God.

→

3. Name some of the present gray areas in the field of morality. How do you handle them?

4. Do you know of someone you would call a "wise person"? What characterizes their wisdom?

twenty-two

an alienated person ...

... accepts without remorse the negative, evil side of life.

Many attempts have been made – serious attempts – to discover the whereabouts of the original Garden of Eden. The only place it will be found is in the minds of Jews of several centuries before the time of Jesus. They, like other tribes and cultures, were seeking for an explanation for their human origin and of why they suffered evil. Their particular exploration, inherited by the Christian tradition, was set in the myth of a Paradise and the Fall therefrom, a story we know so well.

We human beings are the only creators of evil. There is no evil in the animal world because animals cannot make choices. They follow their instincts and perform according to their nature. We speak of some animals treating others with cruelty – the leopard tearing the gazelle to pieces – but this is projecting human behavior on to them. All animals act in accordance with God's will for them. The leopard is doing its leopardy thing. Not so our human species.

When the minds of our earliest ancestors evolved to the point where they were able to differentiate between themselves and all that was around them, when their imaginative faculty developed, and along with it their ability to make personal choices, inevitably disagreements arose. Then arguments, then blows, then fights, then murder.

In the undifferentiated state, the state of the baby in the womb, the state described as that of the Garden of Eden, all is in harmony.

For a baby to remain forever in the safe environment of the womb would bring death. There must be birth as there had to be the "birth" of our ancestors from the non-differentiated to the differentiated state with all the pain that that involved.

Tomorrow's Christians, accepting the theory of how we evolved from lower to higher states of consciousness, realize that in fact there was no one-time Original Sin committed by one pair of ancestors causing humanity's Fall from a perfect to a less perfect state, but there was a breaking out from a womb state to a personalized state.

St Augustine, and even many Church leaders today, would have us believe that we are all born with Original Sin, which we inherit through the sexual intercourse of our parents. True, we are all born into this world with some form of dis-order. We are born into an evil world. None of us is fully integrated, completely whole. We all have inclinations and desires – some inherited, some learnt – for things that do not accord with the model God has given us.

Each religion has its own mythical explanation for the presence of evil and each offers a path by which we can be released from it.

We cannot ignore the fact that we are, every one of us, alienated people. Alienated from our true self, alienated from other people, alienated from our Divine Source. We are in disharmony.

For a disunited people to live together peacefully, our ancestors had to decide collectively what behavior would be allowable and what would not. The unity of the tribe was essential for its survival. As these codes of conduct are about human behavior, we find they are basically the same in all cultures. We Christians derive ours from the Hebrew code. In the Bible this code is given authority by being presented as if given directly by God: the Ten Commandments given to Moses. God gave our ancestors the intelligence to work out this code for themselves. And thus it has continued through history and continues today. As each new moral dilemma appears we have to work out the way to handle it which is the least destructive and most life-giving for all of us.

"Sin" is human-caused evil. Our sense of evil comes from our concept of God. God is unchangeable because change requires time and God is outside time. God just is. Thus our evil cannot affect God. God is neither pleased with our good behavior nor displeased with our evil behavior. He is not a being who loves us more or loves us less on account of our behavior. It is we who cause ourselves and others to suffer. How easy to tell God we are sorry and ask forgiveness and promise amendment: how difficult to do the same to our neighbor whom we have offended. But that is what really counts. That is what heals. There is not a God who punishes us, either individually or collectively, for our failings. Our punishment lies in having to suffer the consequences of our bad actions. Upon reflection, such consequences are a considerable contribution to our learning process. Our greatest hurdle is to forgive ourselves.

It is unrealistic for tomorrow's Christian to imagine that it is ever possible to find perfection in this life. Many people are deluded in this way, thinking that possessions and power are the providers of happiness. Every one of us is in some respect disfunctional. We have to live with that while attempting to function more harmoniously. The evil we do is always, ultimately, a blockage to growth, either to our personal development or preventing the growth of someone else or militating against the evolutionary process of the natural world, Planet Earth, by our destructive greed. We damage the harmonious relationship within ourselves – between body, mind, and spirit – between fellow human beings and between humanity and our physical environment. In doing so we are destructive of the Divine plan for creation. By analogy then, and only by analogy, we can say we damage our relationship with God.

matters for pondering or discussion

1. Do you feel the need to express sorrow to God for your sins?

2. The original Greek word for "sin" is *amartia* which literally means "to miss the mark," as in archery. Are you able to think of "sin" as error?

3. Is there something in your past life that you feel you have not been able to forgive yourself for? Is now the time?

4. Do you understand the difference between moral guilt (your responsibility for an evil act) and psychological guilt (caused by your feelings)?

5. At gut level, are you afraid of the Last Judgment?

6. Do you carry a sense of failure because you know you can never be perfect?

twenty-three

a forgiving person ...

... seeks and accepts forgiveness.

Who of us is fully in control of what we do? Our decisions can never be made in complete freedom. Our so-called "free will" is never completely free. Is a Christian Palestinian youth brought up in Bethlehem, where both of his parents were killed and his house demolished by an Israeli bulldozer, free to embrace Jesus' words: "Love your enemies, do good to those who hate you"? Are the children brought up on either side of the sectarian divide in Northern Ireland uninfluenced in their choice of behavior by the prejudice of their parents? If decisions are not made in freedom, can blame be apportioned? Can guilt be admitted? Can forgiveness be sought?

One day while I was living in Zambia I read in the daily paper that a teacher was up in court and when charged with stealing hens had pleaded: "I didn't do it. It was an evil spirit within me that did it." This might not be our own plea but how often have we felt a moral powerlessness, which causes us to say: "I couldn't help it. Something overcame me." We are all the children of our culture, our situation, the evil in our environment. All these determine our degree of freedom – or lack of freedom – to act.

Yet when we have been offended, we presume the action of the offender was made in complete freedom, with total deliberation. We expect their contrition before we are prepared to forgive.

One of the most frequent teachings of Jesus was about forgiveness.

"Forgive us our trespasses as we forgive those who trespass against us." He saw forgiveness as the measure of the quality of human relationships that ensures that the Kingdom of God becomes a reality. He not only spoke about forgiveness, he practised it. Can we conceive of any less likely situation than that of a man who has been shamed, flogged, dragged as a criminal through the streets, and finally nailed to a cross to die, in his final moments praying: "Father forgive them, they do not know what they are doing"?

Jesus frequently spoke out against injustice, whether practised by an individual or by the system. He displayed anger when he saw wrongdoing, as in his fury at what he saw as the desecration of the Temple (John 2:13-17), but his anger was never directed at an individual. He understood the social forces at work that caused people to act as they did. "Do not judge others, so that God will not judge you" he warns (Matthew 7:1).

There was advice Jesus gave about revenge, which is generally misunderstood: "If anyone hits you on one cheek, let him hit the other one too" (Luke 6:29). He was not saying let yourself be victimized. He was proposing a non-violent confrontation of violence. A person striking another in anger will, if he is right-handed, strike the left cheek. Challenge his anger by inviting him to strike the other cheek. This can only be done with the back of the right hand or with the left hand. Either way, it is not a blow made in the heat of the moment but with deliberation. In other words, cause your assailant to stop and think. Jesus was not saying: "Don't react."

Forgiving and being forgiven are healing moments for both parties. It is hard at times to forgive. To forgive is not to be equated with to forget. To forgive is an act of the will, not of the emotions. Our memories, on the other hand, cannot be eradicated by an act of the will. It is equally hard at times to accept forgiveness. Both to forgive and to accept forgiveness can be heroic acts. Nevertheless, to hold back our forgiveness of another is to hold ourselves in chains, chained to the other. To forgive is to release ourselves. To accept forgiveness is equally a release. When the "woman of ill-repute" washed the feet of Jesus with her tears and anointed them with oil in the house of Simon the Pharisee (Luke 7:36-50) Jesus said: "The great love she has shown proved that her many sins have been forgiven." Her love came from experiencing forgiveness. She did not have to earn forgiveness by first demonstrating her love.

Every one of us has to admit that we need forgiveness. Without this recognition, the forgiveness offered by the offended person will be ineffectual.

The teaching and practice of forgiveness by Jesus is the only way healing can take place, not only between individuals, but between feuding families, sectarian divisions and between political oppressors and the oppressed. And it begins with each of us individually. This is our contribution toward making God's Kingdom a reality in our present time.

matters for pondering or discussion

1. What can we learn about political forgiveness from the Truth Commission established in South Africa at the end of the apartheid regime, when the truth of previous violence was owned and confronted by both the perpetrators and the victims, for the healing of memories and to move forward as a nation?

2. Are you imprisoned by your own inability to forgive the perpetrator of some past injury, physical or emotional?

3. If so, what will be your first step to release yourself?

4. Are you partisan to a group – family, religious, or political – that sees no way out of a situation of mutual hate, suspicion, or mistrust?

5. Is there really no way forward?

twenty-four

an empowered person ...

... regards Jesus' life, death, and resurrection as a liberating of our God-given potential.

I f, as we said in a previous chapter, there has in reality been no "Fall" from a more perfect to a less perfect state – and there is no mention of the Fall in the Hebrew Scriptures, and consequently it would not have been part of Jesus' religious belief – how are we to explain what Christian tradition calls "Redemption"? Certainly not to rectify a past rebellion by an original couple against the Creator, or as a requirement to placate an offended God. Dr. Arthur Peacocke, an ordained scientist, says:

> There is no sense in which we can talk of a past perfection. There was no golden age, no perfect past, no original perfect individual Adam from whom all human beings have now declined. What is true is that humanity manifests aspirations to a perfection not yet attained, a potentiality not yet actualized, but no original righteousness ... Classical conceptions of the Fall and of sin that dominate Christian theologies of Redemption urgently need re-interpretation if they are to make any sense to our contemporaries.

First, we need to understand why St Paul and the other New Testament writers spoke in such terms as:

- God made peace through his Son's sacrificial death

(Colossians 1:20)
- By the death of Christ we are set free (Ephesians 1:7)
- By his sacrificial death we are now put right (Romans 5:9)
- You were killed, and by your death you bought for God people from every tribe, language, nation and race (Revelation 5:9)
- Jesus died outside the city in order to purify the people from sin with his own blood (Hebrews 13:12).

What are the elements common to such expressions? First, the understanding that there is a rift between God and humanity and that this can only be mended by an act of appeasement. Second, the appeasement, the act of reconciliation, is expressed in the sacrificial terms of the times: the need for shedding blood, the killing of a victim. So we are presented with the horrific picture of God sending His son to Earth to die the most horrific death because only in that way could God be satisfied. This is not a picture with meaning for us today. So how did it arise?

Imagine Jesus' closest friends who for three years (as far as we can tell) had given up their job and their families to follow him, who had cheered with the crowds, singing Hosannah as Jesus entered Jerusalem amidst the people waving palm branches, about to acknowledge him as their king. Then within days, his capture, imprisonment, trial, and ignominious death came as the most tremendous shock. Their idol, their Messiah gone from them forever, not in glory but in shame. Their world was turned upside down. They fled in terror; they locked themselves in a room together and grieved. Our grieving is the more intense when it is over some sudden unexpected tragedy. We can only be helped through it by finding some explanation or by imagining what good might come out of it, or simply by persuading ourselves that it is "God's will." For the apostles, an explanation had to be found. They pored through their Scriptures and there in the Psalms and the Prophets they found words that gave meaning to their loss. Jesus was the scapegoat released into the desert bearing all the sins of the people.

He was the sacrificial lamb that had to be slaughtered and his blood spilt to put right the broken God-humanity relationship.

Their understanding, their comfort, was found by looking to the past. But what if there was no past to be healed, no "fallen race," if there was not an offended God demanding his pound of flesh?

It is difficult for today's Christians to break through to a new way of thinking of "Redemption" because the Church's teaching and prayers – using such words as "sacrifice," "salvation," "atonement," "dying for our sins" – perpetuate the backward-looking explanation of the death of Jesus.

So how else might we understand the Jesus event? While teaching that Jesus came to raise us to a new level of life, the Church has never actually, in its two-thousand-year history, defined *how* the life, death, and resurrection of Jesus accomplished that for humanity. Many explanations have been offered down the ages by saints and theologians, which made sense to people of their time. For instance, that God had been thwarted, dishonored by the behavior of Adam and Eve and that therefore a price had to be paid by humanity to make amends. But since no person was without blemish, no one but a sinless Christ was able to do this. Or, in the days when slavery was the custom, the act of Jesus could be described in terms of our being redeemed from, bought out of slavery to sin by a price – the human sacrifice – being paid.

To make sense of it all today, we have to find another explanation. The crucifixion was demanded by human beings, by the religious leaders who felt threatened. It was not demanded by God. It highlights human injustice, not God's justice. Professor Geza Vermes says:

> [Jesus] died on the Cross for having done the wrong thing (caused a commotion) in the wrong place (the Temple) at the wrong time (just before Passover). Here lies the real tragedy of Jesus the Jew.

The explanation cannot be backward-looking – repairing the effect of a Fall – but forward-looking, understanding the whole Christ mystery as empowering humanity to rise to a life in closer union with God. "At-one-ment" rather than "Atonement."

An analogy can help us. We are always drawn to strive beyond our present attainment, physically and intellectually. (Hence the Guinness Book of Records!) But it is a characteristic of human nature to require one of our species to break through the barrier of human limitation in order to empower others to follow. Examples are Captain Webb who was the first to swim the English Channel in 1875 or Edmund Hillary and his guide Tenzing Norgay, the first to reach the summit of Mount Everest in 1953, or Roger Bannister, the first to run a mile in under four minutes in 1954. They were barrier breakers. They opened the way for others to follow and even to surpass them.

Jesus marked a unique leap toward a higher spiritual unity. He not only marked the leap, he made it on our behalf. He was able to do this because, as the icon of God, he was the perfection of humanity, free from the inner enslavement to which we are all held captive, that false ego. He empowered us, not by injecting a new power into humanity from without but by liberating a God-given gift already present but needing to be released.

Thus tomorrow's Christians are shifting the explanation of the Redemption from a negative one of being redeemed from an evil past, to a positive one of the release of our inner creative power to enable us to grow to the fullness of our humanity. We have been empowered to become the complete persons God wills us to be.

mɑtters for pondering or discussion

1. How have you been able to explain to yourself or others the apparent contradiction between a God presented as a loving Father, and a God who demanded the sacrificial death of His Son?

2. How can you be open to receiving the empowerment offered by Jesus, breaking through the barrier of egotism?

3. Are you in any position to replace those hymns and prayers that maintain the Fall-Sacrifice notion by others which are about Jesus empowering us?

twenty-five

a Christed person ...

... believes that each of us is a manifestation of the Christ.

Our present-day worldview, with its acceptance of our place in an evolving Universe, contains two implications. The first is that it challenges a traditional Christian belief that God intervened deliberately at some moment in history to create a human being, a being essentially distinct from any previous creature in that this creature had an eternal soul. Second, it challenges our belief that there was another direct intervention by God at a later point in history when the Second Person of the Trinity "came down from Heaven, by the power of the Holy Spirit, became incarnate from the Virgin Mary and was made man" (to quote the Nicene Creed).

The man Jesus was a product of millions of years of evolution. While there was no need for him to have a miraculous birth in the biological sense, the myth of such a miraculous birth emphasizes the truth that Jesus was a very special person. In what way special? Whatever may have been the view of the Gospel writers, a contemporary way of answering this question is to say that Jesus can be recognized as the first fully mature man in our western culture: a "new man" in whom the highest form of consciousness – Christ consciousness – has broken through. The theologian Edward Schillebeeckx, in his monumental work *Jesus* entitles one of his chapters: "Jesus, parable of God and paradigm of humanity."

I distinguished in a previous chapter between the historical

Jesus of Nazareth and Jesus as the Christ. That Jesus of Nazareth was an historical person living in Palestine at the beginning of our Common Era – AD as Christians designate it – is widely accepted by historians as well as by Scripture scholars. It is about his being entitled the Christ and the relationship of the Christ to the Godhead that has caused theologians from the earliest years of the Church to debate, theorize, and hold Councils. The relationship between the Jesus of history and the Christ of eternity continues to present a mystery upon which I shall try to throw some light. (By "mystery" I mean that Truth which in its totality we are unable to comprehend. We can only enter it piecemeal and appreciate it partially.)

I understand the word *Christ* to have a broad meaning: to be the manifestation of the Divine in creation. What we are considering here in particular is its manifestation in human form. The Christ-life is the life of God lived as a human person. St Paul wrote: "The Christ is the visible image of the invisible God" (Colossians 1:15), and elsewhere he speaks of "the glory of the Christ who is the exact likeness of God" (2 Corinthians 4:4). Dom Bede Griffiths referred to the Christ as "the icon of God."

So the Christian cannot claim that the Christ is only the human Jesus. The Christ is more than Jesus, indeed more than any human person, however Divine that person is conceived to be. Consequently, to say that Jesus is the Christ is not the same as to say the Christ is solely Jesus. In other words, Jesus is the Christ, but the Christ is the Divine however and wherever the Divine is made manifest.

The Christ is God in creation: the creative word, the Logos. So, John's Gospel begins:

> Before the world was created, the Word already existed;
> the Word was with God and the Word was God. From the
> very beginning the Word was with God. Through the Word
> God made all things; not one thing in all creation was made
> without him. The Word was the source of life, and this life
> brought light to all humanity. (1:1-4)

This is more succinctly put by St Paul: "Christ existed before all things and in union with him all things have their proper place" (Colossians 1:17). The Word, the Christ, is God in the role of continuing creator, holding all things in being.

For us human beings, the Christ can never be totally known on Earth because to see Christ would amount to "seeing the Father" (John 14:9), to comprehend the Godhead. As human beings we can only think of God in human terms. We can do no other. This limited human perception of the Christ I shall call "the Christ myth." (A myth is not a non-reality, but rather the expression, through image or story, of a truth that is beyond our total comprehension, beyond verbal description.)

For us as human beings the highest expression of the Christ myth is in human form. It expresses the archetypal image of the fully mature human being: the person as God-like as it is possible for a human being to become – that ideal person who, in our deepest selves, we all aspire to become. So there are many manifestations of the Christ myth. Indeed, every one of us, whether recognizing it or not, is to a greater or lesser extent, at different times, no doubt, an image, a reflection of the Christ: an embodiment of the Christ. This recognition came to St Paul: "It is no longer I who live but it is the Christ who lives in me" (Galatians 2:20) and elsewhere he writes: "The secret is that Christ is in you, which means that you will share in the glory of God" (Colossians 1:27). There are not many Christs but only the one Christ and many manifestations of that one Christ.

The manifestation of the Christ with which Christians are most familiar is in the human person of Jesus of Nazareth. We think of him as the most complete, the most God-like, most God-filled human being. While the Christ pre-existed the Universe, Jesus of Nazareth did not. He "dwelt among us" in one short period of human history. While Jesus lived in Palestine – supposedly for some thirty years – there was not an absence of the Christ within the Godhead during that period! The pre-existent Christ is in the Godhead eternally, without interruption, what we name the Son, the second Person of the Trinity.

Christian tradition speaks of Jesus' coming as the "Incarnation," meaning that the person of Jesus pre-existed time. In an evolutionary perspective, the very first human beings – those primates which evolved into creatures with which we can identify – were the first creatures to develop a self-reflective consciousness, and consequently the first to have the potential to recognize the Divine in nature. In this sense we can say they were the first Incarnation of the Christ. The Jesus event, a million or more years later, was the achievement of humanity reaching its incarnational maturity. Jesus was not a being different in kind from us, launched into our world from some heavenly abode, but a product like us of the evolutionary process, which is why I speak of the Jesus event as a human achievement. And yet, 2000 years later, the rest of us are still striving to evolve to the heights of the Christ myth.

However, the person of Jesus is more than a model of what we might become. In Christian terminology, "Christ" means the anointed one, the specially chosen of God, and called Messiah, Savior. Jesus, by his being the very fulfillment of the archetypal human being, breaks through the barriers of human limitation and thereby empowers us to follow in the same "Way." He was so completely for others, living entirely for the Divine Other, that the Christ nature within him was made manifest to full capacity. The powers he is reported to have exercised – physical healing, spiritual healing, power over nature and material things – he was able to do, not because he was God, but because he was a fully evolved human being "reaching to the very height of the Christ's full stature" (Ephesians 4:13). Luke says: "The power of the Spirit was with him" (4:14). He is the New Adam, in that he is the first to break through to a new level of consciousness, into the next evolutionary step for humanity. Jesus promised us "Whoever believes in me will do what I do – yes, he will do even greater things" (John 14:12). The Kingdom message of Jesus – the very kernel of his teaching – supposes that humanity is, through him, evolving into a new consciousness, a fuller life. "I have come in order that you might have life – life in all its fullness," said Jesus (John 10:10). The Christ, acting in the world as creative energy, initiates our evolution as creatures of the Spirit. "If Christ lives in you, the Spirit is life for you" (Romans 8:10). The Spirit is always the Spirit of Christ (1 Peter 1:11).

What we call the resurrection of Jesus is the symbol of the newly constituted human creature: that state which humanity will evolve into. Just as at our death we shed our human body as being no longer required, so after his death Jesus no longer required his human body, except in a form by which to make known to his disciples that he still lived, though in a higher form of life. Thus his resurrected "body" had different properties from his physical body.

If at some future date archaeologists found the remains of a body in a Jerusalem tomb that could be identified as that of Jesus of Nazareth, it would not make the slightest difference to belief in Jesus as the Christ.

In the Eucharist we celebrate one of the modes of the presence of the Christ, under the forms of bread and wine, without identifying it with the historical, biological body and blood of the human Jesus. We acknowledge that we form "the body of Christ" (Ephesians 1:23) and are called "to build up the body of Christ" (Ephesians 4:12).

As St Paul could acknowledge, we too are Christed, are reflections of the Divine and, because we have an appreciation of being sharers in Divine Life, we, like Jesus, have the potential to call on the Divine energies that are dormant within us all. Tomorrow's Christian lives with that awareness of being a Christ.

matters for pondering or discussion

1. How far and in what way do the ideas expressed above differ from your own thinking about Jesus the Christ? Do you find that disturbing? If so, why?

2. "Your real life is Christ" Paul wrote to the Colossians (3:4). He would write the same to us. What does that mean to you?

→

3. Do you see any indications that over the past 2000 years humanity is gradually evolving toward the Christ, toward becoming the archetypal image of fully realized humanity?

4. What persons do you know of, in the past or present, who shone for you as "another Christ"? What was it about them?

5. What difference has Jesus' birth and death made during the last 2000 years?

twenty-six

a seeking person ...

... is continuously exploring the meaning of faith.

Each Christian denomination claims that its interpretation of Divine Truth, and its proposed way of responding to that, is the right way. None more so than the Roman Catholic Church, which claims to possess "the fullness of Truth." It is not within our human capacity to possess the fullness of Truth. God alone has the fullness. We can do no more than handle Truth partially as truths, as we said in the chapter on *A Mystery Person*.

If we delude ourselves that we possess the fullness of Divine Truth, that we possess the one and only correct understanding of Divine revelation, then we have no reason to look beyond this. If we think that we already possess everything we need for our spiritual journey, then we believe that we can learn nothing more from any other Christian denomination, let alone from any other religion. We have arrived. There is nowhere else to go. Such a position spells death. The spiritual search is over. Not to move on is to stagnate. To stagnate is to die slowly.

Many of tomorrow's Christians are appreciating that no matter how secure they feel in their own faith, there are aspects of the spiritual life that receive more attention in other denominations than their own. They are looking into these and appreciating them. For instance, those whose worship is sacrament- and ritual-centered are learning from those whose worship is Bible-centered. These latter are opening up to the value of a more frequent celebration of the Eucharist.

But further, many Christians, living as they do today in a multi-ethnic, multi-cultural society, are receiving new spiritual insights by learning about other Faiths, especially those from the Far East stemming from the Hindu tradition with its emphasis on meditation and encountering the Divine in the center of our being.

We need to be clear in our minds about the different meanings we give to the word "Faith."

Irrespective of a particular religious tradition, we can say that everyone's life is lived by "faith," in the sense that it is the deepest life orientation of each of us; that which gives our lives meaning. It is not about what we believe (a list of truths) but what we believe in, without which our life would have no bedrock. This "faith" may or may not be adverted to, but nevertheless gives our life its orientation. Carl Jung, when asked in a BBC interview in 1959 whether he believed in God, replied: "I don't believe, I know." Thomas Merton took that a step further: "We believe, not because we want to know, but because we want to be."

If adverted to, it can lead us to a Faith. That is, the assent to a particular understanding of life's meaning that answers the need at this stage of our lives. This will usually be within the tradition of a particular religion or of a quasi-religion, for example some cause to which one dedicates one's life. This will change as our life situation changes. It is quite subjective. Within a Christian context this form of faith is promoted by evangelization or catechesis.

What is often referred to as *the* Faith, on the other hand, is objective. It is the set of doctrines proposed for belief by a particular denomination, often expressed in a Creed or catechism, and submission to it is required for membership. The expression of *the* Faith, however, is not set in stone but requires to be constantly re-expressed in order to be received by a contemporary culture. As Albert Schweitzer wrote:

> Christianity can only become the living truth for successive
> generations, if thinkers constantly arise within it who, in
> the spirit of Jesus, make belief in him capable of intellectual

apprehension, in the thought forms of the worldview proper to their time.

Each of us has to be that kind of "thinker," not leaving it to official religious teachers, if our personal faith is to be meaningful and nourish us in our everyday lives. Many centuries ago the great theologian, Thomas Aquinas, wrote: "People cannot give consent in faith to what is proposed to them unless to some extent they understand it."

That requires that we become perpetual seekers. As the Church, we are a pilgrim people. Carl Jung sounds a warning. He wrote (Letters. Vol. I, 1906-1950): "Science seeks the truth because it feels it does not possess it. The Church possesses the truth and therefore does not seek it." We are a pilgrim people on the road to Truth until we pass through death.

matters for pondering or discussion

1. List those Christian truths that you consider to be non-negotiable to the Christian.

2. Can any of these be re-expressed in a way that is more compatible with our contemporary worldview? How would you re-cast them?

3. If you recite one of the Creeds, with what understanding do you do so?

4. What insights have you gained from other denominations or other religions, which have enhanced your own Christian faith or practice?

5. Would you call yourself a spiritual seeker, or do you have a fear of moving out of the security provided by your present faith framework?

twenty-seven

a free person ...

... takes the risk of parting from a faith scaffold.

The majority of people who desire to develop the spiritual dimension of their lives feel the need to do so in the company of others. They identify with a particular religion. They feel that the path proposed by that religion meets their need for an understanding of life's most fundamental questions: What is life all about? What is our destiny? How do we reach it?

People of different cultures choose different religious paths. Each path has as its aim to lead people to unity with God. Does God really care about which path a person takes? Is God interested in dogma or pomp or ceremony or sacrifices? What God does care about is that we grow in love. It is for each person to choose the path that they feel will be the best to lead them in that direction. It will be a path unique to them. Our religious path is a means to the end, not an end in itself. The common thread running through all religions, their basic truth, their most fundamental law, is that we should love God and express that love by loving our fellow human beings.

For most of us Christians in the West, our path was chosen for us initially by the family into which we were born. Then as adults we decided whether or not this was the path we wished to pursue. Our decision will be governed by the way we have experienced Christianity, which will mostly be limited to our association with the Church, often meaning our association with a particular structure of Church.

For many, Church membership is a stage they go through on their spiritual journey. While some simply cease to participate any longer, because more immediate gratification of their desires draws them away, others experience the Spirit at work beyond the confines of one particular religious system. Faith is not to be confused with allegiance to an organization.

The elements of any religion – its doctrine, its authority structure, its moral code, its ritual – are the scaffold which holds it all together. But for us too, it is a scaffold for our individual lives. Just as a sapling needs to have a stake planted beside it to ensure its straight growth, and is fenced around to protect it, so we in the early years of our spiritual journey need the support of a spiritual scaffold. We need it to enable us to become deeply rooted in our spiritual path.

As the tree grows, becomes firmly rooted and strong enough not to need its support further, the stake and the fence are removed lest they then become a hindrance to the full expansion of the tree. Tomorrow's Christians reach that point on their spiritual journey when they are able to decide what part of the scaffold, the religious structure, is still helpful and what part has now become a hindrance. It is a hindrance when it is no longer growth-giving but becomes a drain on our energies rather than the nourishment it once was. Unless we feel free to make these decisions, our spiritual growth can become stunted, stuck, and even mis-shapen in what should be a natural process of evolving.

Because "grace builds on nature," as theologians say, decisions about the direction our spiritual journey should take are not made lightly. Such decisions presume that we are integrated within, that our energies are unified, that we experience an inner strength. The adolescent Christian has a need for rules and regulations. Without them there is a feeling of insecurity, perhaps even a fear of the consequence of not following them. The mature Christian is able to discern what is helpful and what is not.

Inner strength is especially necessary because the decisions we make about the degree of our membership or our participation in the religion of our choice – our church membership in the case of Christians – will often be met with incomprehension, astonishment, or even opposition within our community.

It takes great courage to let go of the structures, the scaffold, that have been our support all through life and answer the call of the Spirit to enter into an unknown, though attractive, spiritual dimension. John's Gospel (chapter 3) tells us how Nicodemus, a Jewish leader steeped in his religious tradition, had to face this dilemma when he was challenged by what he heard from Jesus. Jesus said that so great was the psychological shift that was required, it was like being born again.

Spiritual freedom comes at a price. But it is a price that has to be paid if we are to be true to ourselves.

matters for pondering or discussion

1. List the elements of the Christian scaffold of which you would not want to be deprived.

2. Do you feel there are some aspects of your life as a Christian at this time that are holding you back from following the path to which you feel attracted?

3. Have you met any opposition from members of your Christian community to your views on church life? How have you reacted?

4. We each have a unique spiritual path, which we are invited to follow. Which direction do you see your own path taking at this point in your life? Does it call for any big decisions?

twenty-eight

a discerning person ...

... distinguishes between values and techniques.

Values concern why we do things. Techniques are about the way we do them.

The Church presents us with both. It provides us with a knowledge of the values by which a Christian is called to live, what are sometimes called the gospel values. And it provides a number of precepts to help us to live by them.

There are two types of values. There are Universal or Absolute values. That is to say they are values recognized by all humanity. They are unchanging. They are values to which we aspire but which we will never be able to acquire in their fullness. Such are freedom, integrity, courage, love, kindness, honesty, justice, beauty, goodness, peace, truth, ... and such like. If we attempt to build up an image of God, it is of a Being who possesses all these to an "nth" degree.

But then there are Relative values, such as the civil laws of a country, the Highway Code, the requirements of etiquette. These are relative to particular cultures and change with time. They are meant to help us to live the Absolute values more gracefully.

The paradigm out of which we live and make our judgments and decisions is rooted in the value system that we have built up during our lifetime. Their seeds were in our upbringing, our experiences, our education, our religion, the company we kept, and so on. The weight we have placed on this or that Absolute value may have changed from time to time as will have the importance we give to the Relative values, how much we let them dictate our life. Who has not driven in excess of the speed limit?!

From time to time we need to consider the values we live by. Are they conducive to our development, our spiritual growth at this moment in our lives?

To assist us to live up to the gospel values, the Church offers us "techniques" or religious practices. That is, certain prescriptions or rituals as a discipline for our lives. We can easily get into such a habit of performing the techniques – not to say into a rut – that we lose sight of the values they represent. A woman I knew was taught as a little girl to say the "Hail Mary" prayer to the Virgin Mary three times every night to pray for her purity. She carried on the habit into adulthood until one day, when she was already the mother of four, she suddenly asked herself: why do I do this? What am I praying for? Why say the prayer three times? The techniques we employ, while helpful at one time, may now have come to the point where they actually have a detrimental effect when it comes to pursuing the values they were meant to promote. For example, most Churches urge their congregations to attend a service on Sunday. What is the value behind this? It is a means, a "technique," to help us to give at least some specific time to God each week, to re-connect with the local Christian community, to nourish our spiritual lives with God's word and sacrament. For some, the carrying out of this prescription, or the fear of sinning by not attending, has become so important that it eclipses the values it is meant to encourage. Even if they have been ill in bed on a Sunday with a high temperature, they have a feeling of guilt and a need to confess their absence. Maybe a person would be observing a higher gospel value if on a Sunday they went to attend to the needs of a sick parent and were thus prevented from their churchgoing. Jesus warned the Scribes and the Pharisees:

> How ingeniously you get round the command of God in order to preserve your own tradition! For Moses said: "Do your duty to your father and your mother" ... but you say:

"If a man says to his father or mother: Anything I have that I might have used to help you is Corban" (that is, dedicated to God), then he is forbidden from that moment to do anything for his father or mother. In this way you make God's word null and void for the sake of your tradition which you have handed down. And you do many other things like this. (Mark 7: 9-13)

Matthew's Gospel lists the "other things like this" when Jesus condemns the Jewish religious leaders for the burdens of the "techniques" that they imposed upon the people, negating the very values they stood for (Matthew 23:1-36).

The "technique" is no more than a means to an end and the end is always that which enables us to give the highest expression of love.

matters for pondering or discussion

1. Jot down a few values, which immediately come to mind as important to you. Why?

2. What is preventing you from living fully the values that attract you most?

3. Is it time to reassess the values you live by?

4. Do you give greater importance to the accomplishing of the Church's prescriptions and practices than to living the values to which they point?

5. Have any of the "techniques" you observe become your slave-master, obscuring the value they are meant to enhance and thus diminishing or negating the value?

twenty-nine

a post-modernist person ...

... bases moral decisions on a sincerely formed conscience.

"Post-Modernism" is the label given to the philosophy, or manner of living, of our times. Much has been written about this phenomenon, but put succinctly it is saying that people today feel free to question everything, even the most fundamental basis of society and the most traditional beliefs. We are experiencing an overload and fragmentation of information, a diminishing of respect for, and consequent guidance from authority, and a move from objective truth to subjective opinion, which is giving rise to a pick-and-mix code of behavior.

This has come about in the western world due to a number of factors, each of which influences the other: universal formal education has enabled people to be more enquiring; our economic sufficiency raises our concerns from day-to-day survival worries to enjoy more leisure, which in turn enables us to investigate a wide range of subjects which broaden the mind; the availability of knowledge on any subject, of scientific matters especially, through the media and the Internet and the opportunity to learn the opinions of the widest variety of people. Add to these, the enormous number of choices now open to every individual. These factors together promote the present trend to lead a life which is more personal, more individualistic, more self-sufficient, from which it follows that we have less regard for the authority of persons and institutions. This gives us freedom of expression and freedom of lifestyle. But also, incidentally, it imposes increased stress upon us.

More aware that we are all citizens of the same world and influenced, through travel and immigration, by a large variety of cultures, we are questioning our own traditional cultural values.

Science, as a universal language unaffected by culture, is no longer believed to be the provider of all answers for our future. Nor is pure rationalism. In fact there is no longer a belief in any certainties, in any truth as absolute. In other words, everything we have relied on in the past is thrown into the melting pot and has not yet been poured out into a new mold, nor, in fact is it ever likely to be. And among the elements of life thrown into the pot is religious belief.

Tomorrow's Christians feel free to question past religious teaching. They want to be persuaded that it is authentic, by which they mean that it relates to how they experience life within the total context of our present world. They are no longer prepared to have life's decisions taken by other people on their behalf, by people "in authority." They want to decide for themselves how they should live and the quality of life they want for their children.

There is a re-emphasis today on the conscience as the final arbiter in the choices with which we are faced. In some languages, in French for example, there is no distinction between conscience and consciousness. Here we are concerned with the English meaning of conscience. When we say that people are conscientious we mean that they listen to their conscience, they live an ethical life. Literally, the word "conscience" means "knowledge alongside" (con-science) as we might think of a guardian angel being a "companion advisor." The conscience is that "still small voice" at the deepest level of our consciousness, which nudges us into a way of behaving in line with our better self. In Christian terms, the conscience has been defined as our homing instinct for the Kingdom of God.

Far from meaning "do what you like" or "let the situation determine the morality," basing our moral decisions on our conscience does presume a formed conscience. One's conscience is formed by sifting and accepting a variety of ingredients and the composite picture they give us. Among these ingredients are our Scriptures and our Church's teaching. There is the Civil Law. Also the advice we receive from others and our own experience, which we must learn to trust. Then there are the opinions of others expressed in discussion or dialogue, as well as consideration of the here-and-now situation in which we have to make our decision. And under-girding it all is our prayerfulness, our openness to the promptings of the Holy Spirit in whatever form this may come to us.

We need to distinguish between our moral conscience, as we describe it above, and our psychological conscience. This latter arises from our feeling guilt. It predominates among children who do not have the maturity to arrive at a formed conscience. For example, if a small boy breaks a window with his football he will feel more guilty if he has broken a big window than a small one. In neither case is he actually guilty of any offence, but his feeling of guilt may arise from the punishment he expects. It has no relation to moral evil.

In these times, which may feel so chaotic and without reliable guidance, we are called upon in our spiritual life to build our personal bridge between religious doctrine – what our Church proposes for our belief – on the one side, and our present-day culture on the other. (By "culture" I mean simply "the way we do things around here.") There is a double bridge between the two. One of these is our language. All religious language is metaphor. It can only approximate the fullness of anything spiritual. The other is faith. The belief system upon which we base our life has to be expressed, even to ourselves, in a language which rings true with our culture. Take the word "grace" as an example. As a religious word it has a particular meaning for us. But how would we convey that meaning to a non-churched stranger at the bus stop for whom "grace" probably implies poise?

Our post-modern culture is calling upon tomorrow's Christians to make a personal shift in their religious life. A shift from accepting religious truths as "given," to venturing to make our own journey of discovery. From relying upon what we are taught, to putting more reliance on what we experience. From the ideal of seeking perfection as "soul business" – saving our souls – to seeking wholeness in body, mind, and spirit, for both ourselves and for others. From regarding opposites (different faiths, for example) as being in conflict, to accepting to live with the paradox of opposites. (If I maintain I am right, it does not follow that the different belief of others is wrong.)

In embracing this new paradigm, tomorrow's Christians may find themselves in conflict with a Church leadership that in many cases is still stuck in a pre-modernist model.

matters for pondering or discussion

1. Does the picture drawn in this chapter resonate with your own experience?

2. Name some recent situation in which you have found yourself acting in conscience in a way that is different from Church teaching. Have you felt at peace about this?

3. How many different meanings can you think of for the word "grace"? How would you explain them to an un-churched person?

4. Do you feel comfortable living in a world where everything is questioned? What assurances would you like to have?

thirty

a new-consciousness person ...

... is aware that humanity is on the threshold of something quite new.

One of the features of the post-modernist times in which we live is that people are feeling free to look far and wide for what they believe will nourish their spiritual lives. This accounts for the plethora of phenomena to which the media apply the label "New Age." The label is applied to so wide a variety of practices, theories, and lifestyles that it is quite impossible to try to embrace all these phenomena in one neat definition. In fact a great deal of what is labeled "New Age" is actually a return to ancient, pre-historic practices. So much has been written about the New Age – for it and against it – that we need not develop the subject here.

Since this New Age phenomenon has come about without any initiator or hierarchical structure, without any unifying ideology or doctrine or any accepted body of authoritative texts, without any headquarters or membership requirement, we might rightly ask what has brought about this "spirituality" that has seeped almost unnoticed into so many areas of our present day culture?

I believe, as do many people, that it is just one of many indications that the whole of humanity is entering a new level of consciousness that is being sparked off in the western world.

Already in 1939 the Jesuit scientist and mystic, Pierre Teilhard de Chardin, wrote:

> At the root of the major troubles in which nations are today
> involved, I believe that I can distinguish the signs of a
> change of age in mankind.

and in 1942 he wrote:

> A great many internal and external portents (political and
> social upheaval, moral and religious unease) have caused
> us all to feel, more or less confusedly, that something
> tremendous is at present taking place in the world.

Many other insightful Christians – Thomas Merton, F. C. Happold,
Dom Bede Griffiths among them – have written in the same vein.
They see the emergence of a spiritual awareness, which is beginning
to govern peoples' lives. By spiritual awareness I mean what has
been described as: "The effect the inner person has on the outer." In
other words, more people are basing their lives on spiritual rather
than on material values. They live out of a deeper consciousness.

These, to me, are evidence of the movement of the Holy Spirit in
our times. Clues to this can be found in three positive features of
today's attitude to life, each of which is feeding the other. The first,
I name "a social awareness," which reveals itself in our concern for
human rights, for justice in our world, for action to overcome the
poverty of people of the Third World, in the spread of democracy,
and in the freedom to hold people in authority – politicians, the
clergy, lawyers among them – to account.

Second, there is the collection of concerns that we can put under
the heading of the "ecology movement." This desire for the well-being
of our planet unites people of all religions. We are appreciating how
Mother Earth is a living organism to be nurtured and not destroyed
by greed. We are viewing our planet in its smallness with regard
to the vastness of the Universe, the totality of God's creation. We
support environmental issues with Green movements.

And third, there are those features of today's life which might
fall under the heading of "feminine values." Namely, the challenge

to the patriarchy that has been our dominant social structure for thousands of years, the concern for building up mutual relationships, the greater creativity among ordinary people, the increasing anti-militarism.

An expression of this last in the Churches is a move away from a military attitude to our spiritual journey – seen as a warfare against the Evil One: "Onward Christian Soldiers" – which stressed the masculine values of self-discipline, order, and obedience, toward a mystical, charismatic spiritual path with its feminine imagery. Its literary idiom is more likely to be poetry than law. It speaks of love, not threats, of self-surrender and resting in God. While the masculine attitude strives for happiness and fulfillment in the next life and offers a prescription for attaining it, the latter seeks unity with the Divine already here and now. The paradigm is changing. A new consciousness is bursting forth.

Tomorrow's Christians live this out in a double dynamic. Outwards, drawn toward relating, toward community, with social concern, dedicated to service of others, attempting to live unconditional love. At the same time, inwards, through such practices as meditation, contemplative prayer, transcending to the still center of our being. Both outwards and inwards nourishing each other, moving us toward humanity's great new evolutionary leap into a new consciousness.

Tomorrow's Christians resonate with the words of the theologian, Thomas Berry, who describes himself as an historian of cultures:

> What is clear is that the Earth is mandating that the human community assume a responsibility never assigned to any previous generation. The human community is passing from its stage of childhood into its adult stage of life. We are being asked to accept responsibility commensurate with our greater knowledge. We are being asked to learn a new mode of conduct and discipline. This is pre-eminently a religious and spiritual task, for only religious forces can move human consciousness at the depth needed. Only religious forces

can sustain the needed effort. Only religion can measure the magnitude of what we are about. ... Our task at this critical moment is to awaken the energies needed to create the new world, to evoke a universal communion of all parts of life.

matters for pondering or discussion

1. List as many manifestations as you have noticed which are labeled "New Age."

2. Mark against each whether it is an ancient practice revived or a new creation.

3. Mark against each whether you consider it to be life-nourishing or life-diminishing or neutral.

4. Have you been struck by any signs of a new consciousness emerging?

5. Have any of these practices or notions been helpful to your own spiritual growth?

thirty-one

an inter-faith person ...

... recognizes that no one religion possesses the fullness of Truth.

During the evolution of our earliest ancestors, their powers of imagination developed and with it the ability to make choices. Unlike any other species, they had developed what we call "free will." Because they had a free will, their choices differed. This led to disharmony in the tribe. How had such an evil come about? How could it be avoided? To answer such fundamental questions the various groups of people developed different explanations, different philosophies of life. Living as they did with their lives linked to the spiritual world, to higher beings, their explanations necessarily were in a spiritual context. They understood their disharmony to be caused by their being out of touch with higher spiritual beings. We have come to call these culturally different philosophies, explaining evil and how to overcome it, "Religions."

Hindus say we are caught in the web of the finite. To be liberated from a cycle of birth, death, and rebirth, we have to find a path beyond finitude to union with the eternal, with Brahman. Jews regard the human family as rebellious, but they believe God intervened in their history to liberate them. They find their freedom in living according to the will of God as expressed in God's Law. We Christians speak of our sinfulness, our separating ourselves from the source of life, as the cause of evil and we believe our way out is by accepting salvation from God channeled through Jesus.

According to Islam we go astray by being forgetful of the Divine nature within. The solution to this is spelled out in the Qur'an. What all major religions (except Buddhism) hold in common is that we have our origin in God and that our final destination is in some form of union with God.If, as tomorrow's Christians, we are spiritual searchers and are open to seek aspects of truth in other religions, we come to realize that no one religion is total, has the complete picture, or can provide the complete package remedy.

It is as if each religion had been given a box of jigsaw pieces with instructions to make the picture. But there is no picture on the box! Some might begin with the edges as an easy way to start. Others would notice clusters of buildings and start there. Yet others might see boats in the harbor and that would be their starting point. At the end of time, each religion will present their completed picture and to their astonishment they will discover that they have all been working at the same picture but each with a different approach.

Each religion is an interpretation of the Primary Revelation, sometimes referred to as the Perennial Philosophy. The Universe, creation, is that Primary Revelation. Each religion interprets it in its own cultural way. The different forms that religions take are their way of making God present to them in their particular culture. Each is a different point of view from which to see Ultimate Reality, so each is a limited expression of it.

Yet there are truths that are accepted by all religions. For instance, the existence of the Transcendent and Immanent, of a Divine Being. Also, that we humans have a relationship with such a Being: a creature-to-creator relationship. That there is a spark of the Divine in all of us. There is a common belief in life beyond death. Further, that we are bound together by a common humanity. We hold so many values in common: love, justice, honesty, mercy, selflessness, faithfulness, forgiveness, trustworthiness, sincerity, truthfulness, peace, care for the Earth ... although our ways of expressing these may differ. As human beings we have a basic common ethic. Each religion enjoys celebrating high points, whether of individual lives or of the year. We have festivals.

To benefit from the insights of other religions for the enrichment of our own Christian faith, we need to approach each, not looking for differences, but in a spirit of dialogue, as we covered in a previous chapter. If comparisons are to be made, they are not to be made between the ideal of our own religion and the lived reality of the other. It is the ideal of each that we seek to compare.

Truth is one. It is eternal. It is an aspect of the Ultimate Reality we call God. But for us in the temporal world, Truth is reduced to a series of truths, differently expressed on account of our historical, cultural, and linguistic limitations. To believe our approach to Truth is right does not mean that another's different approach is wrong. Both are partial. Both are right within their limitations. Accepting that no one religion has the totality of Truth, tomorrow's Christian has her own faith deepened by being open to the ways other Faiths understand the meaning of life and the means they propose for living a more abundant life.

matters for pondering or discussion

1. Do you believe that people of other Faiths are as likely as you to enter eternal life?

2. Make a point of visiting a mosque or temple and ask for an explanation of what you see.

3. Don't be afraid to sit in on the devotions or ceremonies of another Faith, when permitted, without feeling obliged to participate.

4. Name something in the religious practice of people of another religion, which reveals a weakness in your own Christian practice.

5. Are there among your friends people of another Faith with whom you can share deeply life's fundamental concerns?

thirty-two

a celebrating person ...

... is spiritually nourished by Church liturgy.

The normal setting for living a Christian life is as a member of a community of Christians. The local Christian community is a microcosm of the universal Christian community, the Church.

As we all like to celebrate particular events in our lives – birthdays, jubilees – or to mark certain events in the year – the four seasons – so does the community of Christians in a way special to them. Traditionally Sunday has been the celebration day of the week. This pattern is now changing but the need to celebrate is not thereby diminished. But can we honestly apply the word "celebrate" to our Sunday churchgoing? Traditional liturgies often seem so dreary, stilted, and meaningless.

When tomorrow's Christians celebrate it is not with the intention of *giving* anything to God – our praise, our worship, our gratitude. There is nothing we can give God that will make Him more happy, or cause Him to appreciate us more! The value of our praise and gratitude is that it gives us a reminder of our relationship with God.

The late William Temple, Archbishop of Canterbury, summed up worship's purpose succinctly:

> Worship is to quicken the conscience of the holiness of God, to feed the mind with the truth of God,

> to purge the imagination with the beauty of God,
> to open the heart to the love of God,
> to devote the will to the purposes of God.

Yes, worship is for our benefit, not God's.

Some liturgies are very structured, being based on centuries of tradition, and not much deviation is permitted. Other forms of worship are more creative, to meet the needs of particular people on a particular occasion. While ritual carries tradition with it – and this is an important ingredient – a less ritualistic form of liturgy would allow more freedom to express where we are today, to touch the deepest concerns of our daily life.

Sometimes the ceremony is designed entirely by the clergy, other times with lay participation or occasionally entirely by the laity. Worship, liturgy, however designed and carried out, has as its first purpose to enable people to have an encounter with the Divine, to nourish the spiritual aspect of their lives. Liturgy is for people, not people for liturgy.

Tomorrow's Christians seek nourishment for their spiritual lives. Sadly many report that they are not finding this in their local church. What they wish for is that their church-attendance should be life-enhancing, a celebration of the totality of life. They expect it to be a participation in God's communion with the whole Universe. "Worship is not something that happens between the Church and God but between the world and God" says a World Council of Churches document. A liturgy that is spiritually nourishing brings all the different dimensions of life into their relationship with the Christ. Such a liturgy is not "busy" as so much of our worship is. It is not afraid of periods of silence for contemplative meditation. A priority in prayer is that we dispose ourselves to be open to God communing with us. The use of symbols through which our senses are able to play a part, can lift us to a higher form of union than any amount of words.

A good liturgical celebration needs to be built on the foundation of a sound theology expressed in the idiom of our time. It is at once traditional and contemporary. It must offer hope and inspiration, help and guidance, healing and comfort, familiarity and security and, above all, an experience of belonging to and being accepted by the community. Authentic worship arises out of authentic community.

Some of the most nourishing liturgical celebrations are held outside a church building. Many churches with their long naves and rows of pews were designed for a liturgy of a past age, when laity participation and involvement were not invited. Today, participation is expected on all occasions, secular and religious. This calls for a different ordering of the setting, a changed ambiance. Many of our church buildings are centuries old. In some, one senses the presence of the sacred, the aura of generations and generations of praying Christians. Others feel bleak, soulless, perhaps reflecting the fear-inspiring God who has been preached there. Are our places of worship warm (even physically!), light and welcoming, with chairs able to be moved for the occasion, replacing the toast-rack benches? The structure must serve life, not be life-draining by expending energy to preserve a structure that best served an age that has passed.

Tomorrow's Christians select prayers and hymns in the language and thought-patterns of our day. So many prayers and hymns in use in churches today reinforce the theological thinking of a past era and prevent people from re-thinking, re-wording their beliefs. We recall the Latin phrase: *Lex orandi, lex credendi*: "What people pray they believe." No wonder young people think of Christian worship as belonging to a culture foreign to their own.

New thought is being given to ways of communicating the Good News. The sermon is no longer effective in these days of electronic media. People seek dialogue, the opportunity to question, the chance to share their faith stories. The preacher is not the only vehicle by which the Spirit speaks to us. The message of the gospel is eternal and multi-cultural. The ways in which it is expressed, communicated, and celebrated must come across as Good News applicable to our daily life. Otherwise it is neither news nor good.

matters for pondering or discussion

1. Do you have the opportunity of meeting with your fellow churchgoers to evaluate your church services?

2. How might you bring new life into your parish liturgy? Fresh hymns? Re-written prayers? Use of art and symbols?

3. How does your parish bridge the gap between those who enjoy a traditional form of service and those who desire a more contemporary form?

4. Can you honestly call your Sunday service a "celebration" of the Christian community?

5. Does your priest or pastor dictate the style of worship in your church?

6. Make a list of the reasons why you think people are not attracted to come to church or have opted out of church attendance. Does this throw up any suggestions for a way forward?

thirty-three

a meditating person ...

... needs no words to communicate with God.

For many people, prayer is understood as saying prayers. And "saying prayers" is synonymous with asking God for our needs.

An increasing number of people today are seeking places of quiet, moments of stillness in the midst of their frenetic life. More and more are turning to meditation in their search for a deeper prayer life.

We need to make the distinction between two uses of the word "meditation." In western asceticism it is used to describe mental prayer in which the mind ponders on a scriptural passage or inspirational text. This is discursive meditation; it engages the rational mind. It is different from the passive prayer of contemplation, the prayer described as "active passivity." In the eastern tradition the words "meditation" and "contemplation" are used exactly the other way round. When we see advertisements for lessons in meditation, it is the eastern form which is meant. This is what I write about here, the eastern form considered as Christian contemplation.

Although this way of meditating is regarded by some as a New Age practice – and for many it is – in fact it is a Christian tradition going back as far as the monks in the desert in the fourth century and mentioned in *The Cloud of Unknowing* by an unknown English author in the fourteenth century. Sadly the practice has been lost to the western Church for centuries.

There are several ways of helping us to enter into this form of prayer. It may be by watching our breathing or counting our breaths. It may be by focusing the eyes on a picture, a candle, or a mandala. Or it may be with the use of a mantra, a word which itself is not a prayer. All are ways or techniques with just one purpose, to still the mind, to allow God to speak to us. "Be still and know that I am God" wrote the psalmist (Psalm 46:10).

Tomorrow's Christians no longer feel at ease with saying prayers, addressing a God out there with a shopping list! Many feel they have got stuck in their prayer life. It has become a duty rather than a joy. They want to have an experience of God, to enter into communion with the God within. Today we all live such exterior lives. A hundred per cent of our awareness is of or through the body, of material things, of things outside us. To bring balance back to our lives (as we mentioned in an earlier chapter on living by the double dynamic of exterior service and interior stillness) we need to move our consciousness to our inner self, our soul-self, our center point. "No movement in religious life has any value unless it is a movement inwards to the 'still center' of your existence, where Christ is." Words of Pope John Paul II when he visited Ireland in 1979. An Indian spiritual writer and professor of comparative religion, Ravi Ravindra, wrote: "In all spiritual traditions it has been recognized that unless one repeatedly renews one's contact with the center, in meditation, prayer, or quiet contemplation, one is depleted and lost."

This form of deep meditation is of more than spiritual benefit. Being a holistic exercise, it is of benefit to the three dimensions of life that make up our whole: body, mind, and spirit. It is totally transforming. It enables people to live at a deeper level of consciousness and, since all that we do is influenced by our level of consciousness, our exterior action becomes more effective. It is recognized as improving our relationships because we become more loving, we experience a deep unity with other people – the source of our being meets the source of their being – we more easily recognize the Divine in each one. Because we become more centered, more secure within ourselves, we are more able to take the risk of going out to encounter others. Being more in harmony within our own selves, we become less stressed and this in turn affects our physical and mental health.

Furthermore, the practice of meditation not only reduces our own level of stress – and stress is caused by our inability to absorb experiences – but has been found to have an effect on the stress level of our surroundings. For this reason, it is often members of one's own family who become more aware of a change in a person who has started to meditate than the person herself. Many scientific trials over the last few decades have revealed that when groups of people meditate together, the reduction in stress and in the negative consequences of stress in society become measurable.

It is said that meditative prayer is as easy as walking but as difficult as making a pilgrimage. It is easy to do. It demands no physical or mental effort. In fact we simply do it, neither expecting anything nor trying for anything. We let God do the work. Paul wrote to the Christians in Rome: "The Spirit comes to help us in our weakness. For when we cannot choose words in order to pray properly, the Spirit himself expresses our plea in a way that could never be put into words. And God who knows everything in our hearts knows perfectly well what he means" (Romans 8:26-27). The difficult part is being loyal to a daily – preferably twice-daily – practice varying from fifteen to twenty minutes.

Because meditation creates harmony, it is a wonderful means of community building, indeed, of binding together the human community. Swami Paramatmananda (the name given to a Catholic monk, Brother Wayne Teasdale) writes (in *The Heart of Meditation*):

> The spiritual journey is the greatest single resource we have to change the world and bring about the birth of a new civilization that possesses, and is animated by, heart.

matters for pondering or discussion

1. If you feel you are stuck in your prayer life, that it is dry and unrewarding, maybe this is God's way of pointing you to a deeper form of prayer.

2. Jesus said: "When you pray, go to your room, close the door and pray to your Father who is unseen" (Matthew 6:6). The word translated as "room" is the Greek word for the secret treasure chamber at the heart of a Palestinian home. Do you have a "secret" place like this for prayer?

3. If you are not yet a meditator, do you know someone who is who can put you in touch with a teacher?

4. Have you allowed yourself to be dissuaded from learning or practicing some form of meditation by Christians who think it is a dangerous practice?

5. If you meditate regularly and know of others who do, is it possible for you to meet occasionally to meditate as a group? This is so much more powerful in both its personal and its spiritual effect.

thirty-four

a mystical person ...

... realizes that mysticism is not the preserve of the great saints.

"The Christian of the future will be a mystic or he will not exist at all," wrote the famous German theologian, Karl Rahner.

"Mysticism" is not a word in our everyday language, nor even in our everyday Christian language. We associate it with a few chosen saints – mostly of the Middle Ages – who had reached the higher levels of spiritual experience, whose spirituality was manifest by visions, stigmata, or levitation. But mysticism is associated with mystery. It means to see beyond the material reality: to see the presence of the Divine in everything and everyone around. To be able to recognize that in the diversity of humanity – cultures, traditions, religions – lies the creativity of God. But especially it means to recognize and respect the Divine within ourselves. The tenth-century St Symeon the New Theologian (as he is called) wrote: "The greatest misfortune that can befall you as a Christian is not to know consciously that God lives within you."

To be a mystic means to live from the heart, to be centered, to be whole. Tomorrow's Christians are people who are re-connecting with the heart, appreciating the feminine values: emotions, feelings, imagination, intuition. Everyone of us is called to be a mystic.

A characteristic of today's shift in consciousness is a search for spiritual experience, for mystical experience. I mentioned in the last chapter that one of the disciplines that more and more people are adopting, the practical means they are taking on this path, is through perseverance with some twice-daily form of deep meditation.

We are so achievement-orientated in the West that, despite all our good intentions when we begin, we easily give up such a practice if we do not feel it is doing us some good. If we are to invest time in it, we expect results! We forget that such meditation (in its eastern sense) is more than simple prayer. It is a spiritual exercise. It is a holistic exercise that gives nourishment and balance to body and mind as well as to spirit. It has long been a widely accepted Christian axiom that "grace builds on nature." Unless one is integrated within, one's energies are not unified and one is unable to receive and co-operate with the inner work of the Spirit. Effects there certainly are, but they are often very subtle and for that reason they are noticeable only in the long run. As one grows spiritually, it is natural and necessary to be free of that level of religion which is expressed simply in "saying prayers." In clinging to that level, one is stunting the process of spiritual growth.

There are many different meditation disciplines on offer today. One has to find the method with which one feels most comfortable. Whichever method is employed, the purpose of all of them is to enable us to become still, to still our busy minds. As the famous mystic, Meister Eckhart, said: "Nothing in all creation is so like God as stillness."

Those fearful of where this kind of meditation might lead – they speak of the danger of emptying the mind with the consequent danger that evil spirits will take possession of it – point to the Gospels and declare that Jesus never taught a meditation method. However, from the fact that no direct mention is made of such a teaching, we cannot conclude that he gave none. He certainly spoke a great deal about the inner life and the importance of developing it. What we notice is that he offered people the teaching they were ready to hear and able to accept. To his chosen few, his disciples, he imparted a higher teaching. But it is only the former that has been passed down to us in the Gospels because the Gospels were written for the general public. To his disciples Jesus said: "The knowledge of the secrets of the Kingdom of God has been given to you, but to the rest it comes by means of parables" (Luke 8:10) and Mark writes (4:33-34) "He spoke the word to them (the crowd) as far as they were capable of understanding it ... but he explained everything to his disciples when they were alone."

Regular meditation causes us to move into a more real world, or rather, to move about our world while recognizing in it a reality that we had not suspected existed. It is like people born completely color-blind who have grown up knowing only a world of blacks and whites and grays. Suddenly they can see everything in full color. They are seeing the same objects but now recognizing that they have a quality that they had never suspected. In this new vision of reality we appreciate the interconnectedness of everything and experience ourselves as part of that.

When we meditate, we are coming into contact with our deepest Selves, our real Selves, the Selves God intends us to be. The more we meditate the more this real Self is enabled to develop and bit by bit replace the false self. Both in our own Selves and in the new outlook and deeper awareness we have of our surroundings, we are growing from the unreal to the real. And because we are beginning to act out of Reality, we release the energies of the unconscious and all sorts of new avenues are open to us of which we had never dreamed before.

The more we allow our real Self to develop, the more facility we gain for living in the conscious presence of the source of all reality which we name God. As one author wrote: "My true self is a holographic fragment of a Greater Self."

We are surely familiar with those words of St Augustine in his *Confessions*:

> Late have I loved you, O Beauty, so ancient and so new; late
>   have I loved you!
> For behold you were within me, and I outside; and I sought
>   you outside and in my ugliness fell upon those lovely

things that you have made. You were within me and I was not with you.

matters for pondering or discussion

1. Name some people you know whom you experience as living at a deep level, whom you would describe as spiritual people. What is this quality they possess?

2. "I can't empty my mind, however hard I try." How often have you complained of this? No one can empty the mind of thoughts. It is the very nature of the mind to think. What a meditation technique does is to occupy the surface mind so that we transcend to deeper levels.

3. If you are a meditator, can you honestly claim that you practice regularly?

4. What benefits have you found from your practice?

thirty-five

a dying person ...

... regards death as a growth point in the continuum of life.

Despite the fact that each year a hundred million people pass from their Earth-based life to the next stage of their journey, death is a taboo subject for conversation. As someone has observed, in Victorian times when it was normal for people to die at home, surrounded by their families, death was often a topic of conversation, but the subject of sex never was. Today everyone talks about sex but no one likes to talk about death! People are whisked away from their homes to die in hospices or hospitals, often alone. Every possible means is taken to prevent a person dying, to keep them alive as long as possible, even when they have lost all their faculties. It is as if death is the ultimate evil.

Every animal fights to preserve its life driven by its survival instinct. But it is an instinct, not a knowledge. We human beings, alone of all creatures, have the knowledge that we are going to die because we alone have a sense of the future. This is the cause of our fear.

Fear plays a greater part in our lives than we like to admit. Sir J. G. Frazer wrote (*The Golden Bough*): "Men are undoubtedly influenced far more by what they fear than by what they love." Our deepest longing is for completion. Our deepest fear is the opposite, annihilation. Terrorists do not have to destroy their enemy. They just have to inject the fear of destruction into the enemy, then hide. This fear acts like a virus that makes the enemy self-destructive and mass-destructive. This is what we see happening in our world today.

At death, we stand on the edge of where what already exists ends and what does not yet exist begins. This is the end of our past time and the beginning of our future time. We cannot foretell the future. It does not yet exist. But we can and do imagine the future. What we imagine depends on whether we are motivated by love or by fear. We conjure up visions or nightmares. The theologian, Hans Kung, has written in his book *Eternal Life*: "The Church's power over souls ... seemed to be secured better by the fear of eternal damnation than by anything else."

It has been said that what we fear more than the state of death is the process of dying, because dying is the ultimate letting-go. The newly born baby is 100% self-centered. Slowly she comes to recognize that there are other people who have their own needs and a process of letting go of self begins. The whole of life that follows is a slow, and often painful, journey of letting go, up to the point of the ultimate let-go. We came into the world with nothing; we leave it with nothing.

And what then? The fact is that nobody, but nobody, knows because nobody has ever come back to tell us.

Some Christians claim that the fact of the resurrection of Jesus is proof of life after death. But his resurrection appearances – and they were only to those who believed in him – were neither a resuscitation of his pre-death physical body nor of a post-Ascension existence. There is a great deal of controversy among Scripture scholars as to what the apostles and evangelists were describing in the various, and often contradictory, accounts they gave of the post-resurrection Jesus.

The majority of tomorrow's Christians do indeed believe that life does not cease at death but continues in another form, on another wavelength, one might say, without speculating where or how.

The increasing research these days into out-of-the-body experiences and near-death experiences witnesses to the fact that our consciousness has an out-of-the-body and out-of-the-brain existence and is able to "see" things happening around our body with the mind's "eye." Death is a moment of transformation into another state of consciousness. Many of those who practice (eastern forms of) meditation acknowledge that their regular meditating diminishes the fear of dying because while meditating one is moving out of a sense of time and space and just being present to the NOW moment, the God moment. As in dying, one enters into meditation neither with a preconceived idea of the outcome nor with the intention of achieving something. The Christian simply does it to give that time to God, an act of letting-go of our ego. As in dying, so in meditating, we cannot force anything to happen: we just are. As in death the meditator passes from knowing *about* God to knowing God, free of reasoning, free of discursive thought. Intuitive perception will be our post-death way of knowing.

Tomorrow's Christian has no fear of the biblical descriptions of an immediate or Last Judgment, realizing that all are poetic ways, similes, to speak of the unknowable. There will not be a weighing up of all our bad deeds against the good deeds upon the celestial weighing scales, as so often depicted by artists, because all that will matter at the moment of death will be our degree of love. God does not take us anywhere at death: He eternalizes the degree of love we are in at the time. All our earthly life till then is a process of letting-go of our self-centeredness and growing in our unconditional love of other people, the only way in which we can express our love of the invisible Other, God.

matters for pondering or discussion

1. How do you feel about your inevitable final passage through death?

2. What is it that frightens you about it?

3. Do you have the chance of showing concrete and tender concern for the sick and dying?

→

4. Write your own obituary.

5. Compose a meaningful funeral service for yourself.

6. Ask yourself: What is it I absolutely must do before I die? Then do it!

thirty-six

a frontier person ...

... is always open to exploring new avenues.

A frontier is a powerful metaphor. It can represent the boundary where one thing ceases and another begins. Here we can build barriers and dividing walls or we can engage in the growth of relationship. The present moment is that frontier where past time ends and future time begins. It is not time: it is a meeting point between times. It is the edge of creation, where what already is ends and what is not yet is becoming. It is the fiery edge where creation is realizing itself out of nothing. It is where the process of creation is at work.

A frontier is a threshold between the old world and the new. We are leaving the old world behind and stepping into open space where we can build the world of our dreams.

The popular art critic, Sister Wendy Beckett, has said: "Future Christianity is generating itself from the lives of those who have fled to the margins." Tomorrow's Christians fly to the margins, or rather, to the frontiers, not to exclude themselves but to be freer agents to bring new life, more meaningful life, to the Christian community and through the Christian community to the world.

Our original faith paradigm, our religious baggage, was formed by family influence, by our formal education, by our cultural and social environment. It gave us a sense of belonging to a particular Church. It endowed us with a sense of loyalty to our denomination: "my Church, right or wrong" – except that there was no place for the wrong! Then came our encounters with Christians of other Churches, even with people of other Faiths, other cultures, other beliefs and we were faced with a dilemma. Either we were so alarmed by these encounters, because we could not deny the good we recognized in them, that we fled back to the safety, the sure path to salvation proclaimed by our own Church, lest we be deterred from "the straight and narrow path," or we faced up to what we met. For what we met challenged the belief framework of our upbringing. We had to heed our conscience, or rather our consciousness. It demanded answers to some disturbing questions. Are we the only people to be saved? What do we mean by being saved? Is life on Earth really all about getting to Heaven at the end of it? Is God more loving to some people (Christians) favoring us with His grace and less concerned with the other five sixths of humanity?

So with these disturbing thoughts buzzing around in our heads, we felt we had to confront our original faith paradigm. We allowed ourselves to be awakened to a wider vision. There followed a period of exploration and challenge. Disturbing times. The challenge came as much from our fellow Christians as from deep within ourselves: "You are being disloyal." "You are endangering your faith." And even "You are being tempted by the Devil." Then followed, but only after some considerable time and soul-searching, the decision to move to the frontier, to be open to the Spirit in whatever form and from whatever source Her inspiration might come.

With this decision came peace. In moving outside our own traditional parameter we met other like-minded searchers. We met up with tomorrow's Christians!

As we moved forward with them, we discovered that the new paradigm out of which we were now living had a number of consequences besides giving great relief at feeling less stifled.

The word "Revelation" took on a new meaning. It was not just something that happened centuries ago when the Bible was written, but the continual guidance of the Spirit revealing God's action in the world, leading humanity to the full purpose of His creation.

Religion was not the only gateway to the Divine – still less were its priests and ministers God's only spokespersons – but just one source for nourishing the spiritual dimension of our lives. Similarly, the Christian Church in its many forms did not have a monopoly of the Spirit. The Spirit was at work in all humanity, within the Church, outside the Church, and often, it must be said, despite the Church. This was evident in the obvious goodness and deep spirituality we were discovering in people of other faiths, who in so many ways put us to shame in our religious observance. We were growing in a more Kingdom-like attitude to the whole of Creation, coming to realize that we human beings are not outside and above the rest of creation with permission to dominate and use as our greed dictated. We were one with the rest of creation, interconnected, interdependent, given the task of stewardship, of caring for it, of enabling its evolution. We were sharing the vision of St Paul who could write: "The Christ is all, the Christ is in all" (Colossians 3:11). Heaven, we were coming to see, was not a place to which we might one day journey – as distinct from the fearsome "other place" – but is the lived awareness of our union with the Divine in whichever phase of life we happen to be. And of course our relationship with God was changing. No longer thought of as a Being "out there" to be feared, or even as a Father figure, but a close friend with whom we are in partnership to bring about in our surroundings the kind of world that God wants: the Kingdom announced and lived by Jesus the Christ. We were beginning to experience "the glorious freedom of the children of God" (Romans 8:21).

A way to use the book with a group

(The optimum size of a group is between 6 and 12 people.)

The following format is suggested as a way to use a chapter in a gathering lasting one and a half hours. Times given are meant to be no more than a guide and may be adjusted according to the judgment of the person leading.

Begin with a few moments of attunement: e.g. be present to (but do not think about) the fact that each of us is a searcher for a way of living our Christian life in a more meaningful manner.   3 min.

Someone reads the chosen chapter aloud – slowly.   10 min.

A time for each to reflect on it in silence.   5 min.

Without interruption, each person has a turn to share their reflections either on the text or on the questions.   15 min.

A silent time to reflect on each person's sharing.   5 min.

A general, free discussion.   30 min.

A chance to make the sharing our own. Each one writes down:
• What was new for me in what was shared today?
• What was confirmed by what I heard today?
• Has anything I heard today disturbed me?
• Has anything I heard liberated me today?   5 min.

Share with the others as much or as little as you wish of what you have written down.   10 min.

When everyone has had the chance to speak, end with some moments of attunement. Just be aware of how much each of us contributes to each other.   3 min.

Agree a date, place and time for the next meeting and decide which chapter to use.

Sources

Augustine, St, *Confessions*. Fontana Books, London. 1957

Berry, Thomas, *Our Children: their Future*. Bear & Co, New Mexico
   The Dream of the Earth. Sierra Club Books, San Francisco. 1988

Billington, Ray, *Religion Without God*. Routledge, London. 2002

Bonhoeffer, Dietrich, *Letters and Papers from Prison*. SCM Press,
   London. 1981

de Chardin, Teilhard, *The Future of Man*. Collins, London. 1964

Geering, Lloyd, *Christianity Without God*. Bridget Williams Books,
   Wellington, New Zealand. 2002

Holloway, Richard, *Dancing on the Edge*. HarperCollins, London.
   2000

International Monetary Fund, Report on Globalisation. 1997

Merton, Thomas, *Conjectures of a Guilty Bystander*. Burns & Oates,
   London. 1995

Peacocke, Arthur, *From DNA to Dean: Reflections and Explorations of
   a Priest-Scientist*. Canterbury Press, Norwich. 1996

Ravindra, Ravi, *Science and the Sacred*. Quest Books, Theosophical
   Publishing House, Illinois. 2002
   The Yoga of the Christ in the Gospel according to St John. Element,
   Dorset. 1992

Schillebeeckx, Edward, *Jesus*. Collins, London. 1983
   I am a Happy Theologian. SCM, London. 1994

Schweitzer, Albert, *A Place for Revelation: Sermons on Reverence for Life*. Macmillan Press, New York. 1989

Smith, Adrian, *The God Shift: Our Changing Perception of the Divine Mystery*. The Liffey Press, Dublin. 2004

Spong, John, *Resurrection: Myth or Reality?* Harper, San Francisco. 1994

Why Christianity must Change or Die. Harper, San Francisco. 1998

A New Christianity for a New World. Harper, San Francisco. 2001

Teasdale, Wayne (Swami Paramatmananda), *The Heart of Meditation* in *A Parliament of Souls*. KQED Books, San Francisco. 1995

Temple, William, *Nature, Man and God*. MacMillan, London. 1953

Tillich, Paul, *The Courage to Be*. Collins, London. 1952

Tolle, Eckhart, *Stillness Speaks*. Hodder & Stoughton, London. 2003

Vermes, Geza, *The Changing Faces of Jesus*. Penguin Books, London. 2001

World Council of Churches, *The Church for Others*. WCC, Geneva. 1968

Reviews

Today's Christians find themselves in a world that is changing at bewildering speed. For increasing numbers, the old certainties on which they could depend seem no longer relevant. The author addresses this challenge and identifies three very different ways in which Christians attempt to respond. He offers a way forward for those who are looking for a new understanding of Christianity that will help them to make sense of and engage positively with our changing world. The book presents an inspiring and multifaceted vision of "Tomorrow's Christian." The layout with many short chapters makes the book easy to read and digest. I enjoyed reading this book immensely. I find it stimulating and encouraging.

Philip Sheppard of *Christians Awakening to a New Awareness*

The author has given an insight into what future Christians will believe, feel, think, and hope ... and a whole lot more besides. Divided into 36 short chapters, the book fast-forwards several decades, as far as the Churches are concerned, but is based upon what the author knows of those "Tomorrow's Christians" who are already on-board spaceship Earth. Based on the values of Jesus of Nazareth, the book makes clear that "Tomorrow's Christians" will be much more like Jesus than most of those who have lived in the last 2000 years. Those who have already given up on the Churches will be greatly uplifted by this forward-thinking book.

Frank Pycroft of *ONE for Christian Exploration*

For those of us who may despair at the present state of the Church, we look for books that give a clear line without false shortcuts to popularity. I write that because there are those like Adrian Smith who have not lost their wish to proclaim the gospel clearly and in communion with the Catholic elements of the Churches. In *Tomorrow's Christian* he gives clear expositions of the desirable attitudes and aspects of tomorrow's Christian. This book is not for those who want a quiet life. You will be challenged to become a much better and more exciting person to be with!

David Storey of *The Modern Churchpeoples' Union*